DEVOTIONAL COMMENTARY

THE
Image
Maker

dust and glory

Brian & Candice Simmons

BroadStreet
PUBLISHING

BroadStreet Publishing® Group, LLC
Savage, Minnesota, USA
BroadStreetPublishing.com

The Image Maker: Dust and Glory

Copyright © 2019 by Brian Simmons and Candice Simmons

978-1-4245-5926-8 (softcover)
978-1-4245-5927-5 (e-book)

All Scripture quotations are from The Passion Translation®. Copyright © 2017, 2018 by Passion & Fire Ministries, Inc. Used by permission. All rights reserved. ThePassionTranslation.com.

Stock or custom editions of BroadStreet Publishing titles may be purchased in bulk for educational, business, ministry, fundraising, or sales promotional use. For information, please email info@broadstreetpublishing.com.

Cover and interior by Garborg Design at GarborgDesign.com

Printed in the United States of America

19 20 21 22 23 5 4 3 2 1

To our children, grandchildren, great-grandchildren,
and those to come.
You are precious and delightful.
You are our joy and God's spiritual seed.
To each of you this book is affectionally dedicated.

"Don't yield to fear for I am your Faithful Shield and
your Abundant Reward!"
Genesis 15:1

Contents

Introduction

The book of Genesis is God's autobiography. The seal of perfection stamps every word and every page. If you were to combine the skill of all the greatest literary minds, you would never be able to design a composition that equals the splendor of this first chapter. It stands as a masterpiece in a class all by itself.

The whole purpose of creation is to display the wonderous glory of our God. For we see in the created order of our universe the awesome wonder and mystery found in the Maker of all the heaven. The entire universe is his advertisement, for through it, his glory is on full display (Psalm 19:1). The earth is not "mother earth" as it is often called, but instead it's his footstool, and all of heaven is his throne.

> This is what Yahweh says:
> "The heavens are my throne
> and the earth is my footstool.
> Where is the house you will build for me?
> Where is the place where I will rest?
> My hand made these things
> so they all belong to me," declares Yahweh.
> (Isaiah 66:1)

But it is not the earth or the cosmos that is God's highest order. It is man and woman made after his kind—a Godkind of creation. God has created humankind to become a container for his glory. He longs to have the worship of those who love him, freely and with all their hearts. God wanted to create you. He made you as the masterpiece of his creative skill. Everything God created brings him pleasure, even you! He created you for his own pleasure, for you carry his image.

> "You are worthy, our Lord and God,
> to receive glory, honor, and power,
> for you created all things,
> and for your pleasure
> they were created
> and exist."
> (Revelation 4:11)

but This is a totally unselfish way - pleasure - ealous

From the very beginning of time, we see that God is powerful, purposeful, wise, and full of glory. All he has to do is to speak the word of creation from his eternal dwelling place of light and everything comes into being from nothingness (Hebrews 11:3). And so, creation takes us into the mystery of worship where we have no answers to our curiosity; we can only worship. For man's eternal purpose was not to be a scientist, astronomer, or philosopher but a worshipper (John 4:24). That's made so obvious by the fact that we'll never be able to take the mystery out of creation. For a God who is incomprehensible in his greatness accomplished the creation of all things!

Every book of the Bible contains God's secrets. He unveils them to our hearts by the Holy Spirit. The book of Genesis is where God gives away his secrets to the hungry. There is a deep level of meaning embedded in every verse of the tremendous book. Look for Jesus on every page, and you find him, sometimes hidden in metaphor or symbolic speech, but he is there, reaching his arms out to you, his beloved.

The Christian world is somewhat indifferent when it comes to the deeper revelations of God. Some believers have been taught to stay away from them, to basically ignore symbolism and allegory. But I have a feeling that doesn't describe who you are. You're ready to go deep, to look past the letters and investigate the passion of God's heart through the stories of Genesis. The Bible is much like a human being. We have an outward person and an inward person. To know the inward person is what we call relationship, intimacy, friendship, and comradery. So it is with the living Word of God. It requires that we take time and ponder, unveiling our hearts to the mysteries of the Bible. The wisdom hidden in the creation account itself is enough to keep the hungry-hearted ones searching and digging deeper into truth. Don't yield to the thought that you already understand the text. Be alert for something new, something you've never thought of before, and enjoy the discovery that awaits.

I hope you'll take the time to read through this book a chapter a day. It will give you insights into the first eleven chapters of Genesis. We have written this to be a devotional commentary, to give you a vibrant picture of God our Creator, and to discover his gracious love for you! So enjoy reading about the Image Maker himself and how he will shape you and me into the image of his glory.

Brian and Candice Simmons

1

In the Beginning

This is where it all begins—in the beginning. As far back as your mind can imagine, God was there, the only one who has no beginning. Imagine it with me. There was no space, yet his fullness was everywhere. Infinity surrounded him with limitless possibilities. God was able to do anything he desired. And he was fully satisfied with who he was—Father, Son, and Holy Spirit, the one and only true God, God transcendent and God alone. God lacked nothing, yet something was missing.

In time before time, he had determined to create a universe and a planet called earth so he could deposit his very image and likeness into his creation. In his eternal thoughts, he knew it was time to act. It was time to bring into being a universe for his glory. God imagined the cosmos with all its vast splendor. He imagined the spinning orbs of the innumerable stars, galaxies, and the universe. He thought deeply before creating earth with its deep valleys, high mountains, and lush landscape. Then he spoke, and it all began with an explosion of light streaming everywhere!

God's thoughts had already imagined and shaped the largest galaxy and the smallest atom before he created them. With exquisite skill and creativity, God shaped all things by his word and spoke them into being with intricate detail and skill (Hebrews 11:3). God created a dimension separate from his own being. No detail was too small for God as he prepared to unveil his masterpiece of wisdom, his dream come true. God speaks order and goodness into his creation.

The book of Genesis provides the foundation of all theology. He was and is the one and only God, the God of beginnings who loved and loves to create beginnings and new beginnings. And the spirit of creativity was and is over all his works. In fact, we can probably translate Genesis 1:1 to say, "God created beginnings." Father-God loves to start fresh and make all things new. Having many beginnings, the Creator-God continues to create.

I remember a special gift my father gave me as an eight-year-old, inquisitive boy. It was a telescope. Many were the nights I would slip outside after dark, set up my telescope on a tripod, and peer into space, gazing on fuzzy balls of light. I learned about constellations and the many wonders of our universe. It is difficult to imagine that anyone could not believe in our Creator God. He is good, all he has made is good, and he loves to bring delight to his sons and daughters.

Who Is This One?

So, who is this God who speaks the galaxies into existence? Who is this one who gives birth to time? Who is this Eternal

One who is so full of mystery and wonder? His Hebrew name is revealed as "ELOHIM," which translates to "The Ancient One," "The Mighty One," "The God of power," or in ancient Aramaic, "The One over the flames." It is a title that emphasizes his sovereignty and power: "Mighty God." Elohim is the plural of Eloah and occurs nearly 2,600 times in the Bible. Eloah comes from the word ahlah, which means "to worship, to adore" and presents God as the one worthy of worship and adoration. Amazingly, the first name of the deity in the Bible is a plural noun that suggests the Trinity. The Image Maker is a three-fold being who made man as a three-fold being—with a body, a soul, and a spirit. Every human being is a three-in-one just as God is three-in-one. We'll discuss that more later in the book.

CREATION AND THE NEW CREATION

The word "beginning" is actually the Hebrew word for "firstfruits." The Bible begins with firstfruits! God is birthing his firstfruits in creation, and his very life sprang forth from what he created. This was the beginning of beginnings. He poured himself into the creation as firstfruits of his eternal purpose for the universe.

In the six days of creation, we see a clear picture of the spiritual redemption of man, purchased for us by the blood of our Lord Jesus Christ as he brought us to himself. The Father always had our redemption on his mind and in his heart. When the eyes of our heart are open, we can see in the seven days of creation the seven stages we pass through to become God's Sabbath people, the people who find their completion in him and rest in his fullness. Let's look at these seven stages of spiritual growth:

"Empty . . . Formless . . . dark"
The Sinner (Ephesians 2:1–3)

"The Spirit of God . . . swept"
Source of life (John 6:44)

Day 1   "Let there be light."
Spoken work (John 1:1–4; 2 Corinthians 4:6)

Day 2   "Let there be a dome (vault, expanse, atmosphere)."
Separation and salvation (Colossians 3:1–3)

Day 3   "Let the land burst forth with growth."
Spirit of fruitfulness (Galatians 5:22–23)

Day 4   "Let there be bright lights."
Spirit of revelation (Ephesians 1:17)

Day 5   "Let the waters swarm [with sea life] . . . let the sky be filled with soaring birds of every kind."
Sweet worship (Song of Songs 2:12)

Day 6   "Let us make a man and woman in our image."
Sharing in God's life (Hebrews 3:1, 14)

Day 7   "God had completed creating His masterpiece and rested."
Sabbath perfection (4:1–11)

God began his work in us in the darkness, in the chaotic mess of our lives before we came to know and love Jesus Christ. That beautiful work continues to this day, bringing you and me deeper into the image of God. You will never need to fear, for God will always bring to perfection everything he begins. You are heaven's masterpiece, so don't judge the canvas before the Master Artist has finished the last stroke.

LET'S PRAY

Father God, my Creator, Elohim, my wonderful God. I love you. I can see your beauty all around me. Today, I let go of my opinions of who you really are and what you are doing in my life. I trust in you and believe that your work in my heart will continue until the fullness of your image shines through my life. Thank you for not giving up on me! Amen.

Amen!!!

2

CREATION MORNING

*When God created the heavens and the earth, the earth was
completely formless and empty, with nothing but darkness draped
over the deep. God's Spirit swept over the face of the waters.
And then God announced: "Let there be light," and light burst
forth! And God saw the light as pleasing and beautiful;
he used the light to dispel the darkness.
God called the light "Day," and the darkness "Night."
Evening gave way to morning—the first day.*

GENESIS 1:1–5

Nothing can compare to these opening verses in the first
chapter of Genesis. It is a poetic and literary masterpiece! We are
so thankful for the inspired Word of God. Every time we read our
Bibles, we feel the light of God drenching us. How grateful we are
to have the life-giving Word of God.

let's go back and look at the various stages of God's creative acts. The first thing we see is the brooding Spirit of God hovering over the darkness of the surface of the waters. What a foreboding scene! Darkness and confusion cannot dwell in the presence of the Creator God. The wisdom and symmetry of the Spirit of God turned chaos into creation's order (Proverbs 8; Hebrews 11:3). Before God spoke, all was void and formless—and the same can be said of our lives before the light of Christ broke forth into our hearts.

Chaos can never thwart God's plans; chaos merely provides an opportunity for God to reveal his power and glory. The way God created the universe is the same way that he creates order in our lives and makes us over into the image of Christ. Systematically, with the creative Word of God, he brings the beauty of his life out of our dark chaos.

And this same Holy Spirit gently hovered over a virgin named Mary to bring his perfect Man into the world (Luke 1:35). The word swept can also be translated as "to brood" or "to flutter." In Deuteronomy 32:11, this same word describes an eagle gently hovering over its young. In Genesis 8:8–12 and Matthew 3:16, the Holy Spirit is the Dove. Another form of this word in Daniel 7:2 can mean "winds of heaven," reminding us of the mighty rushing wind that gave birth to the church at Pentecost. The Hebrew word for brooding is rachaph. It is the literal term used to describe the brooding of a bridegroom over his bride on their wedding night! Since we are his bride, he loves us with an everlasting love and gently hovers over us.

You will see that the progression of creation moves from the lower to the higher, from the darker to the brighter, from the evening to the morning, like the dawning of a new day. For the Word of God puts light into darkness, land in the midst of sea, air where

there is only water, life on the surface of the uninhabi.
God always starts with form then fills it with fullness! 1
come to bring fullness into our darkness.

	FIRST THE FORM		THEN THE FULLNESS
Day 1	Light & Dark	Day 4	Lights of Day / Night
Day 2	Sea & Sky	Day 5	Creatures of Water / Sky
Day 3	Fertile Earth	Day 6	Creatures of the Land

In nature, it's first the bud, then the blossom, then the fruit. It's first the baby, the adolescent, and then the mature adult. So also it is in grace. Step by step, God releases fullness into an incomplete form. Out of our immaturity, God's grace births his perfection. He will put his finishing touch on you until he unveils the Lord Jesus Christ in you. He is the Philippians 1:6 God! Just as God saw the completion of creation before he finished it, God sees the image of Christ each time he looks at you, even in your immaturity. And God will speak into your life what he spoke on creation's morning.

GOD SAID, "LET THERE BE LIGHT!"

All the planning was over. All the colors, the dimensions of space and matter, the intricacies of design and symmetry—all was prepared and ready to burst forth with creation glory. He could no longer hold back his imaginings. He would now put them on display for all to see. He spared no details, for no detail was too small for him as he prepared the unveiling of this masterpiece of wisdom. Then he spoke light into existence.

And as he released his word of power, the universe began to expand at the speed of light, and it's been expanding ever since.

Nothing can stop this light, for God's kingdom operates according to the principle of an endless increase (Isaiah 9:6–7), not by a power that diminishes over time, but by a power that continues to increase as time passes.

Even in the very beginning, light was the first expression that God released in the earth. "God said, 'Let there be light.' And light burst forth" (Genesis 1:3), and yet he didn't create the sun until the fourth day. Just think about it—before the natural sun existed, there was light! And the light was God himself filling the earth with his presence and glory. It was the very essence of himself, a supernatural light going beyond what man has been able to capture in artificial light. It was the very core of light. It was the light to which no man could come close:

> Yes, God will make his appearing in his own divine timing, for he is the exalted God, the only powerful One, the King over every king, and the Lord of power! He alone is the immortal God, living in the unapproachable light of divine glory! No one has ever seen his fullness, nor can they, for all the glory and endless authority of the universe belongs to him forever and ever. Amen! (1 Timothy 6:15–16)

Think about the power of the Omnipotent Word and the uncreated wisdom behind it. God spoke, and there was an explosion of light that is still racing through the darkness at the rate of 5.89 trillion miles per year! No man was there to hear his decree, yet darkness heard the word of his power and vanished. And that word is still proceeding out of the mouth of God. In fact, everything he speaks accomplishes his purpose. Not one of his words is an idle one.

The beauty of the universe magnifies the Creator. Imagine

this: God's thoughts had already shaped the largest gal. . smallest atom before he ever created them. With exquisite skın and ingenuity, he beautifully coordinated all things and spoke them into being (Hebrews 11:3).

When the Holy Spirit gives us spiritual light and opens our eyes to behold the glory of God in the face of Jesus Christ, we begin to see ourselves in our real position in him. It's in his light that we see "light" (revelation). Spiritual light has many beams and prismatic colors: revelation, knowledge, joy, holiness, and life. And all of them are waiting for us to see them in and through his glorious light.

Since light is so good, we can ask our Creator for more of it, and in receiving light we receive more of him, for he is our true light, and he longs to give himself away to us. But there is a necessary division, for light and darkness have no communion. God has divided them so that there would be no confusion between the two. Sons of light must not have fellowship with the deeds, doctrines, or deceits of darkness. For in Scripture, we're called children of the day, and we must be full of light. We must be able to discern between the precious and the vile to maintain the distinction that the Father placed between the two upon the creation of the world that first day.

This light God called "pleasing" or "beautiful" (Ecclesiastes 11:7). God's plan is truly beautiful. He chose the light and separated it from darkness, calling the light "day" and the darkness "night." This is a picture of the Lord Jesus Christ himself, the Light of the World. When Jesus came into the world, the Father said of him, "You are my greatest delight." God called his true light his greatest delight!

THE NAME OF YAHWEH HIDDEN IN GENESIS

The Hebrew verbs used with "Let there be . . . and so it happened" are both related to the holy name Yahweh. Yehi means "Let there be," and wayhi means "and so it happened." When connected, they give us the name of God, Yahweh. In the very beginning of the Bible, Yahweh is mentioned. Yahweh is the "I am that I am," the God who said, "Let there be . . . and so it happened."

It's not difficult for God to work where there is darkness, chaos, and confusion. Man wants to begin with light, but God begins with darkness. He will begin with evening and turn it into day. This is the way God operates.

LET'S PRAY

God, your light spills into my soul today, healing me and soothing me. I thank you that my darkness will not hinder you. You turn darkness into day, chaos into order. You have done so many miracles in my life. Keep working in me until you can flow effortlessly through me. I long for more of you, Father, Creator, my God. Amen.

3

THE SUPER-DOME
OF THE SKY

And God said: "Let there be a dome between the waters to separate
the water above from the water below." He made the dome and
called it "Sky," and separated the water above the dome from the
water below the dome. Evening gave way to morning—day two.

GENESIS 1:6–8

I have always been fascinated by the sky. I love watching clouds
and can often imagine a shape or figure of an angel as I look at the
wind-swept clouds above. Even the night sky seems to draw our
gaze upward to the luminaries of the stars and the moon. I thank
God for his creation and the breathtaking wonder of his glory in
the heavens.

On this second day of creation, God separated the waters below from the waters above (Psalm 33:9; 148:4). He stretched out this "dome" (atmosphere) and named it "sky." The Hebrew word translated "separated" is similar to "spreading a sheet" or "drawing out a curtain" (Psalm 104:2). The clouds wrapped up the waters above. God preserved above us great store-chambers of rain, snow, and hail (Job 28:22–23; Psalm 104:13).

The height of the heavens reminds us of God's supremacy and the infinite distance between us. The brightness of the heavens reminds us of his purity and glory. The vastness of the heavens teaches us of the immensity and grandeur of his majesty. He is the God of the heavens who has stretched out this dome over us.

God loves to make a difference, to separate and put in order. He separated day and night, and here he separated waters above from the waters below. As creation proceeded, there was one separation after another, yet he can also take the parts and make the whole into one as needed (1 Corinthians 12:17–20).

THE THIRD DAY

And God said: "Let the water beneath the sky be gathered into one place, and let the dry ground appear." And so it happened. God called the dry ground "Land," and the gathered waters he called "Seas." And God saw the beauty of his creation, and he was very pleased. Then God said, "Let the land burst forth with growth: plants that bear seeds of their own kind, and every variety of fruit tree, each with power to multiply from its own seed." And so it happened. The land flourished with grasses, every variety of seed-bearing plants, and trees bearing fruit with its seed in it. And God loved what he saw, for it was beautiful. Evening gave way to morning—day three. (Genesis 1:9–13)

Good stuff always happens on the third day! The earth began as a planet covered by a dark, uninterrupted ocean. Suddenly, the Lord spoke, and light shone as the atmosphere took its place. God parted the waters and formed the oceans, lakes, and rivers by the raising up of dry land (Psalm 104:9). On the third[1] day, God created earth's vegetation. For the third day represents the day of fruitfulness and maturity.

God raised the earth out of waters and clothed it with life. In a place of desolation and death, fertility is a God-created capacity. He is the author of life, fruitfulness, and reproduction. Life is in the seed. God's fruits all multiply themselves. The Hebrew for "each with the power to multiply from its own seed" is actually "seeding seed."[2]

Life sprang forth.[3] And as God formed the earth, he brought into being a profusion of flora that could reproduce and cross-pollinate, "each with the power to multiply from its own seed." The earth began to take on this innocent and distinctive character, "and God loved what he saw, for it was beautiful."

The work of God at creation involved three separations. He separated the light from darkness. Then he separated the waters above from the waters beneath. And finally, he divided the water from the land. Out of this separated, resurrected land, God brought forth a variety of life—and that was just the third day!

THE FOURTH DAY

And God said: "Let there be bright lights to shine in

space to bathe the earth with their light. Let them serve as signs to separate the day from night, and signify the days, seasons, and years." And so it happened. God made two great lights: the brighter light to rule the day and the lesser light to rule the night. He also spread the tapestry of shining stars and set them all in the sky to illuminate the earth, to rule over the day and to rule over the night, and to separate the light from darkness. God loved what he saw, for it was beautiful. Evening gave way to morning—day four. (Genesis 1:14–19)

On the fourth day, our eyes turn to the heavens as the Father of Lights creates the great luminaries of the universe. God spoke, and the sun, moon, and stars instantly appeared. What indescribable power!

> God's splendor is a tale that is told;
> written in the stars.
> Space itself speaks his story
> through the marvels of the heavens.
> His truth is on tour in the starry vault of the sky,
> showing his skill in creation's craftsmanship.
> (Psalm 19:1)

Everywhere you look, you can see the splendor of this wondrous setting created by our Father for the objects of his love. Earth is unequaled in its uniqueness. The heavens contain the embedded codes of God's glory. Symbolic signs testify to his greatness and wisdom. This is the imprisoned splendor of God manifested in this sacred universe. For those with eyes to see, the earth contains a hidden dialect of the heavenly language—a language that

one day would become a man, for everything points back to this
one glorious man, Jesus. When perceived, these covert codes
inspire us to have fellowship with this Image Maker.   Yes ! ! !

It is more than a play on words that the sun is a picture of the
Son. He is called the "sun of righteousness" (Malachi 3:2) who
"will rise with healing in His wings" in order to gladden our hearts
and set us free. Here are a few examples of this symbolism from
Scripture:

- The sun is like a "bridegroom" coming out of his
  chamber (Psalm 19:4–6).

- At Jesus's transfiguration, radiant light poured from his
  face like the brightness of the sun (Matthew 17:2).

- The "woman" [church] of Revelation is clothed with the
  sun (Revelation 12:1).

- He is our "Dayspring" (2 Corinthians 4:4).

The moon, deriving all her light from the sun, is a picture of
the church reflecting Christ. The fountain of her light is hidden
from view, for the world can only see him as the church reflects
his beams to a darkened earth.

Scripture often uses the stars as a picture of believers or ministries who shine with light (Daniel 12:3; 1 Corinthians 15:40–44;
Philippians 2:15). We see from Psalm 147:4 that as God named
the "sun" and "moon," he also gave names to each of the stars. And
"He set . . . them all in the sky to illuminate the earth" (Genesis
1:17).

God loves to give us signs. Every day is a parable. The way the
sun and moon and seasons change all paint a picture for the newly
created man. The day becomes a hint of God's ways. He makes
us young in the morning as the sun rises. We become strong and

valiant at our noonday. We become gentle in the calm evening of our lives. Then we hardly know it as the night comes and carries us away, waiting for the next-day resurrection.

Yes, we are the lights God set as a sign to mark the movement of others into maturity. As we become his bright sign, we will begin to "govern the night" by facing the Son and allowing his undimmed brightness to shine upon us. In day or night, the lights can rule and govern. Our lights must shine so bright that they begin to govern over the night and shine into earth's darkness. Every season becomes a journey as we brightly shine as "signs" in and to the darkness.

LET'S PRAY

Father, you are my light in my darkness. When I feel like I'm surrounded by darkness, your beauty-light shines even brighter. I love how you move me into greater glory. Let me see your beauty and your splendor, undimmed and brilliant. Bathe me in your light. Let the light of your glory shine on me and through me today! Amen. *Amen!*

4

Let There Be Life!

God said: "Let there be life! Let the waters swarm with sea life, and let the sky be filled with soaring birds of every kind." God created huge sea creatures and every living creature that moves of every kind—swarming in the water and flying in the sky, according to their species. God loved what he saw, for it was beautiful. God blessed them, saying: "Reproduce and be fruitful! Fill the waters of the sea with life, and the earth with flying birds!" Evening gave way to morning—day five.

Genesis 1:20–23

The God of power brought forth life as his creation work of the fifth day was to give birth to animate life. God created all life in the sea and air: marine life and birds.

This fifth day reveals the work of the Spirit and the ways of

God. On this day, God created the eagle and the dove. Creation proceeded from one level to the next, systematically, as God's order and life continued to flood into his creation until the day of perfect rest.

All things came to life through the Word of God. We often say God created out of nothing. But God didn't create things out of nothing; he created everything out of his Word. He took the substance of the Word of God, which was invisible, and made it visible. Elohim took what had never been seen before and made it known.

> Faith empowers us to see that the universe was created
> and beautifully coordinated by the power of God's words!
> He spoke and the invisible realm gave birth to all that is
> seen. (Hebrews 11:3)

With chaos as his canvas, the Word came and split emptiness open to be filled with his creative commands. Everything we now see was once the Word of God. Everything is a word from his mouth. Even you and I. All your chaos will become his canvas. The endless Word can bring light and life to your mess, for his Word is now in you.

God desires to have one like himself. The Image Maker has a longing to share his great mysteries of eternity. The best is yet to come!

THE SIXTH DAY

God made all things without our help. On the sixth day of creation, God supernaturally created the animals, both wild and domesticated. Species of every variety filled the earth. How glorious and diverse is our God! What love went into the world God created for us!

Can you imagine the delight in the Father's heart as He created the various forms of life? It had to be a fun day! God made every cat and every dog, every kind of horse and cattle, every wild tiger, and every hippopotamus. He put horns on some, spots on others. What fun! The Creator wanted life to fill his creation. It wasn't barren rock and hills but full of life. In every barren place of your heart, you can expect God to create something new and good and beautiful.

> God said: "Let the earth produce every class and kind of living creature: livestock, crawling things, wild animals, each after its kind."
> And so it happened.
> God made the wild animals according to their species, livestock according to their species, and all the creatures that creep along the ground according to their species. And God loved what he saw, for it was beautiful. (Genesis 1:24–25)

God was filling the earth with life, and he loved what he saw. Life is precious and beautiful. Life is to be valued and esteemed. Every life, every person, is precious in God's eyes. After creating the animals, God surveyed his work and knew there was something still lacking. He had trees and their kind, animals after their kind, but there was no "God-kind" of being. He wanted to shape a creation masterpiece that would, in a measure, replicate him. He wanted to embed his likeness and his image into beings that would reflect his glory.

It all reflects the glory

27

Then God said: "Let us[4] make a man and a woman in our image[5] to be like us. Let them reign over the fish of the sea, the birds of the air, the livestock, over the creatures that creep along the ground, and over the wild animals."

So God created man and woman and shaped them with his image inside them. In his own beautiful image, he created his masterpiece.

Yes, male and female he created them. (vv. 26–27)

Shaped by Love

At last, God made man in his own image. Everything up to now was just God preparing for the universe to hear, "Let us make a man and a woman in our image to be like us." This is more than a hint of the Godhead. Father, Son, and Holy Spirit shaped man inside and out!

We are made after God's kind. Imagine the Father's heart pounding as he considered the possibilities of his divine idea. I imagine him saying, "Let us make one we can share our love with!"

The origin of man is strikingly different from the origin of animals. In Psalm 8, David informs us that God has made man to be only a little lower than 'Elohim,'[6] our Creator! The phrase "in our image, to be like us" speaks of both the outward and inward aspects of mankind. The image refers to something inward; the likeness refers to something outward. God has made every human being in his own image and in his own likeness. He has placed honor upon us as the offspring of God, leading us all to the humility of being human.

What is this image God gives to each of us? It includes

personality, the capacity for worship, the ability to make moral decisions, our conscience, and the ability to reflect God. Created as his image bearers, all human beings bear the expression, the image of God. We are photographs of God. Our characteristics were meant to be copies of God's.

Because even fallen human beings retain the image of God, we must do all that's in our power to protect the value and dignity of human life, from conception to the grave. Each one of us is an image bearer sent from the breath of God to the earth.

Our natural human bodies are of this world and literally made from the dust of the earth. Spirit God fashioned the elements of the earth into a super intricate design of a living, functioning mobile house in which our spirits and his Spirit can dwell. We are spirit beings who inhabit a fascinating body with an intelligent sensitive soul that functions seamlessly between the body and our human spirit. And provided in that is a place for the Spirit of God to abide and function in this world.

There is no other creature on earth with this intricate design. God created only mankind to house his Spirit on earth. Not only did the Creator design the human being to house the Spirit of God, but we are also the living vehicle through which God implements his desired works upon the earth.

As the Spirit of Christ becomes one with our human spirit, Christ becomes the head of our entire spirit, soul, and body. The Spirit of God in us connects directly with the throne of God to receive spiritual guidance and empowerment from heaven into our human spirits. Our human spirits then impart the endowment from God into our souls enlightening our minds, wills, and emotions. This in turn motivates the body to carry out the works of God from heaven into the world. This is the way God rules on earth. He rules through his children.

Because he desires to give himself away to you, he took his own nature and likeness and fashioned a creature just like him, one he could love with unlimited passion. Together we are meant to enjoy each other in the warmth of mutual love. Freely and openly we can share our lives and express our hearts. You are his inspiration, formed by his loving thoughts. You are his divine idea.

LET'S PRAY

Father of all creation, you are my Abba, my loving Father. You have shaped me in love to be yours. I give my life to you. Fill me even more with your image until I shine like a light in this dark world. Make me into your complete likeness. I want to be your dream come true. Amen.

5

CLOTHED IN THE GLORY

What is man that you would even think about him,
or care about Adam's race.
You made him lower than the angels for a little while.
You placed your glory and honor upon his head as a crown.
And you have given him dominion over the works of your hands,
for you have placed everything under his authority.

HEBREWS 2:6–8

Jesus's inflamed desire for you is beyond knowledge or analysis. He drinks of your love, feasts on your adoration, and is moved powerfully by your worship. He lacks nothing, yet you complete him. He needs nothing yet longs for more of you. The splendor of God is that Jesus finds delight in the immature and incomplete ones, watching with ecstatic joy as we grow up into the image of

31

Christ. You are his photograph, and when you have developed, you will look exactly like the One you worship.

God desired a partner. Before he could complete his eternal plan, he wanted a partner who was like himself and one in his image. You are that partner! He wants you to walk with him and to work with him in releasing his glorious image into the entire universe.

On the sixth day, God-partners stood before him. Perhaps it was a flame of beauty that surrounded Adam and Eve in their innocence and purity. Crowned with glory and honor, Adam and Eve stood as king and queen over all creation. A shimmering innocence was their only garment. What is the full meaning of creating "in our image"? The incarnation and life of Jesus Christ fully expresses that image. "He is the divine portrait, the true likeness of the invisible God" (Colossians 1:15). The invisible God became visible in Jesus Christ! And since God created man in his own image, and the image of God is Christ, God created man in the very image of Christ.

God gives us our very life. Our Father united flesh and spirit, joining us to both worlds. Formed out of dust yet receiving the breath of God, man became the centerpiece of God's creation. Made a little lower than angels, every human being has stamped upon him or her the very image of the Triune God. To be made in God's image is an invitation to intimacy with the Image Maker. You have the capacity to be one with God. What glory and honor God bestows upon each one of us! *So amazing & humbling*

GOD'S LAMB

Before God formed man, he had a Lamb. And his Lamb was slain before the foundation of the world (Revelation 13:8). God

*O Lord — when You created A & E
You knew they would disobey — how did Yr
heart stand it
Eternity so different from earth.
Hmm*

had our need in mind as he spun galaxies into the sky. Before the foundation of the world, there was a slain Lamb (1 Peter 1:19–20). The print of the nails was upon him as he formed the world, and the hands that formed each person were nail-pierced. As God shaped Adam from dust, he stamped redeeming mercy upon him. The marked Maker has held every life in his hands.

One day, this Creator took on the likeness of man (Philippians 2:6–8). What a wonderful mystery this is! "Emmanuel," God became one of us, a human—like the man he created (Matthew 1:23). This shows that human beings will be transformed into the full image of Christ. Because we have this divine life as a spiritual seed within us, we can be and we will be conformed into the image of Jesus Christ, our Creator (2 Corinthians 3:18; Romans 8:29). And those who believe that Christ is the image of God will be transformed into that image! *Hallelujah!*

God made us to have fellowship with him. For the deep desire of God was to commune with his image bearers (Psalm 42:7). The likeness implanted within us at creation was the capacity to live like Christ. He is our new self. And the One who created us continually renews us into his likeness, giving us the full revelation of God, knowledge after the image of our Creator (Colossians 3:10).

God honors man and woman by giving them charge over all the earth (1 Corinthians 3:22). God made us his representatives to express God and to reign over his creation. He gave human beings this commission of responsibility for exercising dominion over every living creature. The Creator meant for man to rule over "all the things that move along the ground," including the "serpent and scorpion," which represent powers of darkness (Luke 10:18–20; James 3:7–8). This is so all creation could see his image. God desired a man who would take dominion of the earth for God's glory. Only then would the Creator be satisfied. But notice, Genesis 1:26 states, "Let them reign."

The dominion of the earth will only occur as men and women together exercise their proper roles and reign. Both men and women reflect God's image. There must be a joining of the male and female personalities to exercise God's ultimate purpose for ruling over his creation. *Thank You!*

The Lord created for Adam a companion who was not only suitable for him but also one who powerfully expanded man's creative capacities. Indeed, the woman brought many new graces into Adam's world that did not formerly exist, the foremost of which was the power to conceive and give birth.

It is important to remember that God created male and female in his image, according to his likeness (Genesis 1:26). Of course, in certain ways, both Adam and Eve as individuals possessed reflections of the divine nature. They each could think, speak, dream, and create. However, it was in the union of Adam and Eve, in their mutual respect of one another's strengths and graces, that mankind would possess a more perfect expression of the fuller nature of God. *wholeness completeness Thank you again*

The original plan of God included giving his man-and-woman combo the scepter of ruling and reigning. The pathway of co-regency was the path God wanted man and woman to walk on. But it can only come to pass as we incorporate the Word of God into our nature and love begins to reign in our heart. We are the favored sons and daughters of the Highest, wearing his regal robes.

All of creation hinges over the response of man, as a free moral agent, to yield to the Maker. Will we draw our hearts closer to God, or will we depart from him? It's up to Adam. Will man realize his potential in bearing the image of God, or will he ultimately drown in his weakness, bringing the entire world down with him?

> And God blessed them in his love, saying:
> "Reproduce and be fruitful! Populate the earth
> and subdue it! Reign over the fish of the sea,
> the birds of the air, and every creature that
> lives on earth." And God said: "I give you every
> seed-bearing plant growing throughout the
> earth, vegetables, and every fruit-bearing tree
> with its seed within itself. They will be your
> food. They will also be food for every animal
> and bird, and every creature that moves on the
> ground—every creature with the breath of life."
> And so it happened. (vv. 28–30)

God's blessing upon the human family implies love. God blesses both men and women, empowering them to live on this planet, infusing them with power and favor to succeed in life. The Father's blessing was not merely for them to achieve maximum personal pleasure in the garden, but rather he told them to live to impart to the next generation. They were to have children and extend the garden relationship to the nongarden part of their world. They were to pass on the favor of heaven to the next generation. Their purpose was to build into the future and increase until they subdued the nongarden part of the earth.

As they bore children and multiplied the image into other parts of the earth, then the glorious rule of God through man would also cover those places. Sadly, Adam and Eve chose to live for themselves at the expense of the future generations.

God "blessed" them, even after their fall, affirming them in his love. This blessing is what the heart cries out for today. We long for the blessing of our earthly father, but in reality, our true longing is for the blessing[7] from the One who abides forever. Imagine God speaking over Adam and Eve the blessing of a Father! They had no earthly father, only a heavenly one. Perhaps this blessing on Adam and Eve gave them powers we know nothing about. Perhaps part of this blessing of dominion was the power to speak to the earth and food would come forth. It was only after the fall that man labored to farm and till the ground. *interesting*

God gave both man and woman the command to care for the earth and subdue all things. Man and woman, blessed by their Creator, had authority to rule with him as co-regents. Both men and women reflect God's image and his rulership. *Yes !*

The blessing of God is so incredible! Do not underestimate what it meant for the Creator to bless man in the garden. As for God, his work is perfect. He sees all that his hands have made and declares it to be "beautiful," especially the work he is doing in you.

Although God disclosed himself faintly in creation, he has fully displayed himself in his Son (John 1:18). His new creation today is in the believing heart (2 Corinthians 5:17).

> God surveyed all he had made and said, "I love it!" For it pleased him greatly. Evening gave way to morning—day six. (Genesis 1:31)

LET'S PRAY

What a wonderful Father you are! You are more to me than any earthly Father could ever be. Let me hear today your words of life, your words of blessing over me. I long to be near you, even as Adam and Eve walked so near and dear to you. Draw me closer, my Father of Glory. Amen.

Yes! Amen!
Only You have words of life!

6

THE SEVENTH DAY

And so the creation of the heavens and the earth were completed in
all their vast array. By the seventh day, God had completed creating
his masterpiece, so on the seventh day, he rested from all his work.
So God blessed the seventh day and made it sacred, because on it,
he paused to rest from all his work of creation.

GENESIS 2:1–3

God can do a lot in a week. So perfect is God's handiwork that
nothing can be added to it and nothing taken from it (Ecclesiastes
3:14). The morning stars sang together on this glorious day. Like
an artist finishing his masterpiece, God "rested from all His work,"
setting apart the seventh day as a special day for himself.

"And so . . . the heavens and the earth were completed in all
their vast array." The Hebrew text actually uses a word for warfare

when describing the "vast array." It infers that the arrangement of the heavens above contains power. Even the prophetess Deborah spoke of the stars fighting for Israel against her enemies (Judges 5:20).

After God's demonstration of miraculous creative power, God paused. He rested. God was not weary, but he simply rejoiced in his masterpiece. God's work in us, for us, and through us continues through time. God's last day of creating (sixth) is man's first day. As soon as man was created, he rested with God. In this way, he became one with God, dwelling with him and resting in his accomplishments. There is no mention of evening and morning completing the seventh day, for God's Sabbath rest endures forever, and there is no night there. We find our true Sabbath rest in the finished work of Christ. God did not need a Sabbath; omnipotence never grows weary (Isaiah 40:28). God simply rests in himself. This is his own Day[8], and he is satisfied.

The seven days of creation hint at the seven stages through which one passes to become fully mature in Christ, complete in his image. Once we lived our sinful, empty lives in spiritual darkness (Ephesians 2:1–3), the Holy Spirit brooded over our souls to draw us to salvation (John 6:44). Then God spoke his word of power, cascading revelation-light into our being (2 Corinthians 4:6). The Savior, Jesus the Word, is the Light of salvation (John 8:12). Finally, we cease from our own striving and enter into the Sabbath rest of completion and maturity (Hebrews 4:11).

This seventh day is a picture of God's satisfaction with the work of his Son. A holy rest comes to those who trust in Jesus and cease from their own works (Romans 4:5). The seventh day is the realm of his fullness and perfection. God wants to make us his Sabbath rest, his holy day. There is a Sabbath people in the earth today. And they're learning to cease from their own works and letting God implant within them the passion to do what pleases him (Hebrews 4; Philippians 2:13).

Are you a Sabbath rest for God? Can he find a resting place in you? God works in many but rests in few. Where his will rules, there will be rest. If our will is in competition with God's, there will be turmoil.

This was the order: God worked, then he rested. Man rested with God. In this realm of the Father's rest, man is able to work effectively and creatively. If we are outside of that place of rest, we disrupt our creativity, and our work turns into sweat. But in the rest of God, there is never sweat or burdensome toil.

Man's work was an expression of creativity as he rearranged and joined himself together with the natural elements of his Father's world. Creativity became an act of worship, and man joined with God in the garden. Not a forced labor camp (like much of the religious world) but a garden of pleasure where creativity flourished.

The Father gave humanity the keys to artistic creativity. Inspiration flowed through the first couple in the garden. The Creator did not place them in an environment of heavy rules and regulations. He gave them the power of purpose and the freedom to express that purpose through their work.

This is what our God desires: to dwell with man and be at rest with him. In this, man becomes one with God, dwelling with him, and resting in God's accomplishments. Within this Sabbath realm, all is of God. God did not command man here in the garden to keep the Sabbath, but he gave the commandment to Israel at the giving of the Law at Mt. Sinai (Exodus 20). The Sabbath practiced by Israel was just a type and shadow of the reality of Jesus Christ (the true Joshua). He will lead us into that promised land of rest from our enemies.

Jesus once said to his disciples, "And why would you worry about your clothing? Look at all the beautiful flowers of the field. They don't work or toil, and yet not even Solomon in all his splendor was robed in beauty more than one of these!" (Matthew 6:28–29). They don't work or toil. So, within you, the divine nature of Christ-life springs up through the power of his tremendous promises (2 Peter 1:4). God had the church in mind even as he created the universe.

SEVEN DAYS AND THE SEVEN LAST WORDS OF JESUS

The last seven words of Jesus Christ on the cross seem to describe the seven days of creation. The old creation died with Jesus that day. For his death satisfied the justice of God in every respect and made possible the dawning of a new day:

1. "Father, forgive them, for they don't know what they're doing" (Luke 23:34).

When Jesus spoke these words of forgiveness, the shining Light filled fallen hearts. Our lives had no form. They were empty, just like the world before creation. Just as it was in the beginning when God created natural light to dispel natural darkness, he created spiritual light in the person of his Son to destroy the darkness of sin. Just as the Holy Spirit hovered over a formless, empty, and cold planet, so now he hovers over humanity calling us to Jesus, the light of the world. And where does it begin? With forgiveness! The first words from the cross open the human heart to the light of the gospel, and our new life begins.

2. "This very day you will enter paradise with me" (23:43).

On the second day of creation, God separated the waters. On the cross, the second saying of Christ was separating the pure from the defiled, the saved from the lost. Two thieves were crucified with him, but only one heard these words.

3. "Mother, look—John will be a son to you" (John 19:26).

The third day of creation was filled with seed bearing plants. On the third day, resurrection life bloomed. So Jesus speaks of a new relationship and the transferring of the "seed" from Jesus to John.

4. "My God, My God, why have you deserted me?" (Matthew 27:46).

The lights of holiness filled the sky on the fourth day, and it was holiness that came in between the Father and the Son as Jesus became sin for us. Even the light of the sun hid from the sight of Christ suffering in our place.

5. "I am thirsty" (John 19:28).

Jesus thirsts for the nations to come to know him. God created the great waters (seas of humanity) on this fifth day. This prefigures Christ's passion to be the redeemer of all the world and every nation.

6. "It is finished" (v. 30).

On the sixth day, God finished his work and said that his creation "was beautiful and pleased Him greatly!" Jesus finished the great work of salvation at Calvary, and on the sixth day the Image Maker completed his prototype, Adam. God finishes what he begins. "He shaped them with His complete image inside." And today, the Holy Spirit comes and fills us even more as we conform to his will.

7. "Father, I surrender my Spirit into your hands" (Luke 23:46).

Jesus found his rest in the Father, and the Father can now find his rest in the Seventh Man (John 4:17), the perfect Savior. We can find rest daily from sin because the Lord Jesus has completed the work and committed himself (and us) to the Father.

Yes, the Image Maker delighted in this man and woman that he made. And he is delighted in you as you come to his Son and commit your spirit to him!

LET'S PRAY

Jesus, you were there in the beginning, loving and creating and moving in power. Now you are present in my heart, loving and creating and imparting more of your beauty into me. I thank you for the awesome power you displayed at creation and the awesome power you release into my heart today. Thank you for always being kind and powerful in me. Amen.

Thank You Lord for desiring me! My whole life I have desired to be desired & it never happened! All this time - You HAVE DESIRED me!!! At last, I am home in You!

I am soaking in Your delight!
Zephaniah 3:17 The Lord your God is in the midst of you, a Mighty One, a Savior Who Saves! ⌐

He will rejoice over you w/ joy; He will rest in silent satisfaction and in His love He will be silent & make no mention (of past sins or even recall them; He will exult over you with singing: "I am my Beloved's and He is mine," He desires me Intensely! Hallelujah!! Thank You Lord!!! Elohim desires me!

THE CREATOR'S KISS

The man came alive—a living soul!

GENESIS 2:7

God was ready to begin his divine idea. He had formed the man, Adam, out of clay to be a vessel, a container to receive his breath, his very life. And it would all begin with a kiss. Can you imagine someone kissing you into life? When God breathed into Adam's nostrils, it is a euphemistic way of saying that God kissed Adam. Let him kiss me too!

There was no grain in the fields, for there was no rain and no man to till the ground. The word for ground is adamah (similar to Adam). God created the perfect environment for man to take dominion and be instrumental in the flourishing of the earth under God's blessing. So the Lord created man to walk with him and cultivate a garden. God made the earth to need man's touch. God and man were to work together to subdue, cultivate, and take dominion of the earth.

> The heavens belong to our God; they are his alone,
> but he has given us the earth and put us in charge.
> (Psalm 115:16)

In the beginning of creation, God had not yet released rain upon the earth. The book of Joel chapter two allegorizes God's Spirit as rain. God wanted to co-mingle himself with man by his Spirit, but God had not yet sent his heavenly rains, his Spirit, to the earth. When the rain falls, it soaks into the ground (the dust) and mingles with it for producing life.

When Holy Spirit came, man (dust) and Holy Spirit (rain) co-mingled, and God's life filled us. God and man joined together, singing in the rain and working the ground for a harvest. If there is no rain of the Spirit, it is only because the soil of our hearts is still unbroken.

Subterranean streams or a "mist" came up and became the water supply of the earth before the flood. Another accurate translation of the Hebrew word mist is "enveloping fog, or veil." God tore the veil and formed a man.

Everything else God formed by an act of speech. Only man did God create with his hands. The word formed means "to press, mold, or squeeze into shape." We are truly the clay, and God is the Potter (Isaiah 29:16; Jeremiah 18:2–6; Job 10:8–9). God, the Master Craftsman, formed "the man" (HebrewAdam) from the dust of the ground (adamah). All of us come from the dust. This helps put our life into perspective, doesn't it? Our natural and chemical origin is that of dust or clay, not gold. We are to be vessels, not ornaments.

Some miracles begin in mud. You are a walking miracle, and God continues to change our muddy mess into a miracle that will reveal his glory. One day Jesus picked up some earth, spit on it, and made mud, and he touched the eyes of a blind man with it. And the blind man saw! How many of us today would get in *that* prayer line? The prophet told Naaman to go dip into the muddy Jordan River to get healed. He came up a muddy, healed man. Yes, some miracles begin in mud, so don't fear if the mess within you is as great as the mess around you.

God creates every one of us as a three-in-one being, just like himself:

- Body – "scooped up a lump of soil"

- Spirit – "blew into his nostrils the breath of life"[9]

- Soul – "the man came alive—a living soul!"

The breath of the Almighty has imparted to us a living spirit capable of spiritual understanding (Job 32:8) and a functioning conscience (Proverbs 20:27). The "inbreathing" of God produces human life. This is what constitutes humankind made in the image of God. This divine kiss was the catalyst of creation—the breath of the Image Maker. This celestial substance gave life, enabling man to live in a new dimension and able to be transported into the realm of God. In this spirit-dimension, man would have fellowship and intimacy with the Image Maker.

The Father kissed his son and filled him with his breath as Adam's newly formed body surged with the spirit-wind within him. Instantly, every portion of Adam's being filled with life as celestial substance poured into the man of clay lying in the Creator's arms.

Out of the dark shadows of nonbeing, a new life came forth, and a spirit was created. And man arose out of his darkness into the majesty of the light of God's presence. God's divine idea was now looking into the eyes of the Image Maker. Adam's existence began in the very presence of the one and only true God.

Every human being, like Adam, receives the breath of the Almighty at the time of conception. We were all born in the intimacy and love of a creative moment. We looked into the face of God, our Image Maker, in the instant of our birth. We have our Father's eyes!

"The man came alive—a living soul." The joining of spirit and flesh forms the soul of man. God's powerful breath went into a human body and formed a soul. Adam was able to live by the breath of life, which is the spirit of man. Adam is standing halfway between two worlds. He has a body of flesh like the animals but a spirit of life from God. The body links him with the created world and his spirit with the uncreated God. We have a vessel for our journey in time (body) and a vessel for our journey into eternity (spirit).

The Hebrew word for breath or wind is ruach, the spirit-wind of God. Yet ruach can also mean "inspiration" or "courage." When the spirit-wind blows upon us, we receive the courage of life, the passion of God. To be filled with the light of the Lord, the Spirit of God (Ephesians 5:18), is to be filled with the breath of God that gives courage. What's the point of having power if you're too timid to use it?

It takes courage to live the passionate life of God. Adam's courage-wind enabled him to step out into the adventures of God. It's always good to have the power to accomplish our small dreams, but like Adam, we all should desire to have the courage to step out into God's dreams and to see the adventure of our shared life with God unfold.

The first two chapters of Genesis paint a colorful and captivating picture of what it means to be human. It may help to frame our portrait of humanity with two words: humility and honor. Reflecting the image of God, we all have value and significance that exceeds any other creature. However, so that we don't ever forget where we came from, God named his firstborn Adam, "taken from the dirt" (in Hebrew, adamah).

Every time Adam heard God call his name, he remembered that he was only well-designed dirt. Scientists tell us that our bodies are mostly water. Dirt and water thrown together make a pile of mud! No matter how wealthy or cultured we may become, apart from Christ, we are really nothing more than cultured clods of dirt. How wonderous is his love for man! God takes clay vessels and pours his life and Spirit into you and me.

There's a God-given connection between each of us and the earth. We're made from the earth, but we're also made to rule over the earth and care for it. When Adam sinned, it was the earth that became cursed. As we go, so goes the earth. We're earthlings, made to live on this planet. It is only after our resurrection with Christ that God instructs us to set our hearts and minds on things above, on heavenly things. Our co-resurrection with Christ has now made us heavenly beings with a spirit living in two worlds. One world we are to subdue, the other is to subdue us!

Have you ever thought of the immense job God gave Adam? He told Adam to "reproduce" and "be fruitful." "Populate" the earth and "subdue" it. The earth is very big. What a task God gave to Adam! Would God give him a task he could not complete? No, God made Adam and gave him the "breath of life"—a powerful anointing. Before Adam fell into sin, the Creator granted him great powers. All of these powers were greatly diminished after the fall. They are still resident within man but hidden and immobilized:

- Physical strength – Adam never grew weary. Only after the fall did God say he would "sweat" in order to eat. God commanded Adam to work the garden and take care of it. The Garden of Eden had no boundaries. It was limitless.

- Great intellectual powers – Adam memorized the names of countless animals with all their subspecies. God created him with an organizational, administrative capacity that enabled him to identify and define the world around him. As the father of mankind, Adam introduced order and structure to the human experience.

- Authority – Adam took dominion to rule over all the earth. God would not have asked Adam to manage and dominate the entire earth unless Adam had the ability to do so.

- Spiritual similarity to God – God made Adam in his likeness and in his image. This newly created man was a portrait of God. The fullness of this is not yet known but will be one day.

- Created to be a creator – God was inspired with an idea, then God breathed into man. He inspired man and gave him the power to speak, think, plan, implement, create, imagine, build, and love. These are identical traits of the Image Maker. God gave himself to man.

Our imaginations create our worlds. As long as God is the source of this inspiration, our actions bring pleasure to our Creator. And freedom, as a gift from our Creator, releases creativity into the created order.

God created a man to till and work the garden, accomplishing God's purpose for man—to bring forth fruit. But Adam needed a bride, a partner for life who would be able to live and move and be one with him. So God gave Adam a job and a wife! All of this was to be a picture to Adam of God's yearning for a forever partner who would not only work with him but would also love and cherish him.

Let's Pray

Father God, I delight in being your child and knowing that I am your forever partner. I love to serve you, but I love to love you even more. Increase my love for you. Let it spill out into every relationship I have. I want to be your divine partner, your divine idea. In Jesus's Name, Amen.

8

THE GARDEN OF DELIGHT

Then Yahweh-God planted a lush garden paradise in the East,
in the Land of Delight; and there he placed the man he had
formed. Yahweh-God made all kinds of beautiful trees to grow
there—fruitful trees to satisfy the taste. In the middle of the garden
he planted the Tree that gives Life and the Tree that gives the
knowledge of good and evil.

GENESIS 2:8–9

After God made Adam, he immediately gave him a home. Mankind's first home was the perfect setting for Adam—a model home—furnished with love, freedom, creativity, all in the environment of acceptance and peace. God placed all under Adam's custodial care.

The place God appointed for Adam was not a palace of gold

but a garden planted by the Lord on the third day. All that God provides for us is pleasurable. Eden means "pleasure" or "delight" and is the birthplace of delight and desire. The whole earth was a paradise to man, a pleasurable garden, a wonderland. This is life at its highest perfection. Man and woman lived above sin, sickness, pain, and death.

Eden's very name reveals God's nature of love and grace. Even the location of the garden was sweet: "in the east." The Bible commonly uses "east" in connection with Jesus. The east is the place of the rising light. Every time man looks to the rising sun he is unconsciously reminded of his original home. Ezekiel says the Prince will come through the eastern gate (Ezekiel 43:1–4). The wise men saw his star in the east (Matthew 2:2).

The description of the garden with numerous geographical references proves it was more than a mythical place. It was a real and literal garden. God's dwelling place on earth was the Garden of Eden, but one day, he will dwell with us in the New Jerusalem, the City of God. Notice the parallel between the Garden of Eden in Genesis and the City of God in Revelation:

Eden in Genesis	The City of God in Revelation
The River of Eden	The River of God's throne
Gold in the land	Gold in the city
The tree of life	The tree of life
Bdellium and onyx stones	Precious stones
God walking in the garden	God dwelling in the city

Scripture also shows the paradise of Eden, the Garden of God, as a picture of our relationship with God. He continues to love and comfort us today, making us like Eden (Isaiah 51:3). In the Song of Solomon, God calls the bride (the church) his garden (Song of Songs 6:2). Overcomers receive the privileges of dwelling in a glorious paradise-like relationship (Revelation 2:7; 2 Corinthians 12:1–4). Something in every human being longs for this place called Eden. It's the soul's pure delight. Jesus is our Garden of Eden, and we are his sacred Eden (Song of Songs 4:12–15).

The Hebrew word Eden is a homonym that can mean "a plain (steppe)," or "enjoyment, bliss, pleasure, delight." A bliss-filled paradise became the home of Adam and Eve. Eden's very name reveals God's nature of love and grace (Song of Songs 4:12–15; 6:2; Isaiah 51:3). Eden is the realm of glory and bliss that God wants to unveil to the believer. Ezekiel called it both the Garden of God and the Mountain of God (Ezekiel 28:13–16).

Eden is the Kingdom of God, the Holy of Holies, Zion, the place of his absolute Lordship. Though God placed man in a garden, God meant for him to be a garden. Man began in a garden, sinned in a garden, and was driven out of the garden. Then Jesus came. He went into a garden as the perfect man and tasted the fruits of our suffering and pain (Matthew 26:39) that we might become the garden of his delight.

The trees God planted in this garden were the best and the choicest. Everything was a pleasure and delight to man, charming the eye and touching the soul. God was a tender Father to his first son of the earth, Adam. On all sides, discovery and encounters awaited him. God prepared Adam's environment to disciple him in understanding and choice. With joy and gladness, Adam communed with his Maker.

God set man in a garden. Not in a factory where he was to toil, not in a school where man was to study, but in a garden, a place where life grows. Our life in God is to be a garden where beautiful fruit springs forth. And in the middle of the garden, God planted two trees and put Adam in front of the tree of life. He didn't give Adam a list of commandments, but he offered the man living food that would sustain him.

God's purpose for man is not in doing but eating. God presented himself to man in the form of food, for Jesus Christ is that tree (Psalm 1). He is meant to be the life and sustenance for all whom God has formed (John 6:57). The tree of life is the tree of God's uncreated life. Adam was created; he did not have uncreated life like God has. Eating of this tree would transform Adam from the natural into the supernatural, from one created by God to one born of God. The Lord gave Adam the opportunity to forsake his created life, unite himself with God's life, and live in surrender to his life every day. By eating of the tree, Adam would daily show his dependence on God.

The tree of life was to be a seal to Adam, assuring him of the continuance of life and happiness, leading him to immortality and everlasting bliss. As God planted the tree in the earth, so the Almighty implanted his breath within Adam. The Lord planted the tree in the garden, in the ground, and in the dirt. What was man made from? The Lord wanted to plant himself in the dust of Adam and become life within him. A tree planted in a garden and God planted in man is the picture the second chapter of Genesis presents us.

As the soil nourished the tree, so the Maker was to supply life and sustenance to Adam. Life for Adam depended on what he did with the tree. Life for you and me depends on what we do with the tree on which Jesus died. Jesus Christ is now to us the tree of life and is accessible to all who come by faith (John 15:1–8; Hebrews 10:19–20; Revelation 2:7; 22:2).

THE TREE THAT GIVES THE KNOWLEDGE OF GOOD AND EVIL

To eat of the second tree would give man the knowledge of good and evil but without the knowledge of God. These two trees confronted man with a choice: to yield to God's will with a "yes" in his spirit or to reject God's will with a "no," choosing to know him or to know good and evil. Man is not meant to covet knowledge apart from a relationship with God. God longs to be the source of life, virtue, and wisdom. As we come humbly to him (our tree of life), he will feed us and guide us. His wisdom is a tree of life to those who taste her fruits (Proverbs 3:18). Seeking knowledge apart from him will only reveal our nakedness.

The tree that gives the knowledge of good and evil is likely a merism for "the knowledge of everything." The great need of the human heart is life (relationship), not knowledge. Jesus Christ is that living tree.

THE CROSS IS THE TREE OF LIFE

"You had Jesus arrested and killed by crucifixion, but the God of our forefathers has raised him up" (Acts 5:30).

"He himself carried our sins in his body on the cross" (1 Peter 2:24).

Scripture refers to the cross of our Lord Jesus Christ as a tree. God planted the tree of life (Genesis 2:9). Man planted the second tree, the cross. "They crucified Jesus" (Matthew 27:35). It was human hands that Jesus formed, and it was human hands that shaped and erected that cruel cross on the hill of Calvary. We can use the Scriptures to investigate the roles these trees play in our salvation:

- The tree of life was "delightful to look upon" (Genesis 3:6). The "tree" on Calvary was quite hideous, shocking to the senses (Isaiah 53:2–3).

- The tree in the garden released sin and death (Genesis 2:17). The cross brings life and salvation.

- By eating of the fruit of the tree, man lost spiritual life. By eating of the fruit of the cross, the Son of Man, he obtains eternal life (John 6:53–54).

- Both trees were planted in a garden (19:41). The first Adam and the last Adam were buried in a garden.

- Adam, the thief, through eating fruit he stole from the tree, lost Paradise. The repentant thief, through eating of the second tree, entered Paradise. Isn't it more than a coincidence that we find "two thieves" connected with the second tree also? Jesus only used the word "paradise" here as he accepted the thief into his kingdom (Luke 23:43).

- Both trees were "in the middle" (Genesis 2:9; John 19:18).

- Both are trees of "the knowledge of good and evil." The cross is where we see the true knowledge of what is good and what is evil. Jesus personified goodness, and he became sin for us. We can see both holiness and wickedness as we gaze upon the blessed tree.

- Satan did everything he could to get Adam and Eve to eat of the first tree, but he does everything he can to keep mankind from eating of the tree of life, the cross of Calvary.

LET'S PRAY

Father God, I feast on the tree of life today. You are my everything. I long to be filled with your fruits, your love, and your power. I eat of you, and I cherish every thought I have of you. Feed me until my cup runs over. You are my Garden of Delight, my Paradise. I want to feast and find my joy in you alone. Amen.

9

THE RIVERS OF EDEN

Flowing from the land of Delight was a river to water the garden,
and from there, it divided into four branches. The first river,
Overflowing Increase, encircles the gold-laden land of Havilah. The
gold of that land is pure, with many pearls and onyx found there.
The second river, Gushing, flows through the entire land of Cush.
The third river, Swift Flowing, flows east of Assyria. And the fourth
is the river Fruitfulness.

GENESIS 2:10–14

What a beautiful scene: a garden paradise with trees abounding and a flowing river! This was a supernatural river of life with four tributaries flowing through the Garden of Eden out of one source. God wants a river to flow out of you and me, his garden (John 7:37–38).

Most rivers flow into one, but these rivers flowed out of one. Jesus is the source of that river, the river of life. He gives refreshment and satisfaction to the hearts of his own (Ezekiel 47:1–12; Zechariah 14:8).

Psalm 1:3 compares the blessed man to a tree planted by rivers of waters (a reference to Genesis 2). Rivers of flowing waters also created (planted) the man of Eden. God made man out of river-soaked earth. And in the heavenly paradise there is a river that proceeds out from the throne of God and of the Lamb (Revelation 22:1). If you follow the river to its source you will find the Lamb upon the throne. This river is the outflowing of God, the living Word (Psalm 36:7–9; John 4:14).

The tree of life refers to the receiving of divine life, while the river of life speaks of the outflowing or giving out of God's life. Nothing can flow out of the river that hasn't first flowed into it. We can only minister out of that which is flowing into us. Lord, make me a reservoir of this divine water!

The names of the four rivers found in Genesis are Pishon, Gihon, Tigris, and Euphrates. Here are the Hebrew meanings of the names of the rivers and where they flow:

Pishon means "overflowing increase, flowing free, spread out." It surrounds the land of Havilah,[10] and that name means "to cause to grow" (Ezekiel 47:9, 12).

Gihon means "bursting forth, to gush as a geyser, to give birth." This river flows through the land of Cush, a name meaning "blackness."

Tigris means "rapids, swift flowing." It flows past the land of Asshur (Syria), translated as "successful." Euphrates's name means "breakthrough" or "fruitfulness."

These four rivers describe the ministries of the children of

God as they become overflowing with the life of God on the earth. All these rivers combined make up the New Testament life of the four Gospels, as you can see here:

1. Pishon – God's people will overflow the twisting and corrupt ways of man and cause the true life to grow in overflowing increase in the earth. Joy submerges the land of sorrow.

2. Gihon – They will break forth in the darkness of this world system with life-giving streams. The people of light shall encompass the whole land of darkness.

3. Tigris – The children of delight will be swift flowing to show the religious systems and earthly success to be the vain, empty inventions of men in comparison to the flow of life through the Son of God. The release of the river will bring divine life and release to the captives.

4. Euphrates – God's people will rush forth with true spiritual fruitfulness and touch all the earth with the fullness of Christ.

When we interpret together the names of the four rivers, we read: "The River of God will bring overflowing increase, gush like a geyser to swiftly bring God's people to success and fruitfulness." Does that sound like an unfulfilled, unhappy, joyless life? There is a life waiting for you flowing from Eden's rivers of joy. Drink in the joy, and release rivers of life into the world!

Gold, Pearls, and Precious Stones

The gold of that land is pure with many pearls and onyx found there (Genesis 2:12).

Not only was the garden a lovely place but it was also a land of rich minerals and potential wealth. Wherever the river flowed, its waters uncovered gold and costly jewels. God was generous to give these valuable treasures to man in the garden.

The gold was of the purest quality. God often commanded his people to use pure gold to serve him, such as for the mercy seat and the lampstand of the ark of the covenant. Wherever the life of God flows within us, it brings in the gold of his divine nature. God's churches are to be golden lamp stands.

In addition to gold, the river also held the durable and valuable onyx stone. In the book of Exodus, God instructed his people to mount twelve onyx stones to the breastplate of the High Priest, representing the twelve tribes of Israel. This prefigured the twelve apostles, the foundation stones of the New Jerusalem, as well as the onyx that will adorn the gates of that city (Exodus 25:7; Revelation 21:19–20).

The flowing of the river also produced pearls. A pearl is a transformed substance and is a picture of regenerated man (Matthew 13:45). Oysters in the deep waters produce pearls. It's out of a wound to the oyster, such as when a grain of sand causes the oyster's life-juice to flow, that the pearl forms. The forming of the pearl points us to Christ, the Divine Wounded One, who went into the waters of death and secreted his life over us—those who wounded him—to make us into pearls of great price.

The gold, pearls, and precious stones are all transformed substances. And they point us to the work of transformation within our hearts and the image of God coming forward in redeemed man. In Genesis, these substances are lying in a garden. In Revelation, they are built into a city. The New Jerusalem will be a city of gold, pearls, and precious stones, God's holy people. Between the garden and the city, a long process must take place.

LET'S PRAY

Father, how beautiful and wonderful you are! Your rivers of delight pour into me and out of me into the world. I love being the container of Christ. May living waters flow from you to me. I ask for more of your rushing, flowing life to come through me and touch my family. I want the rivers of God to run though me into this dark world. Do it today, Lord. I open my heart to receive your life-giving flow. Amen.

10

FAVOR AND FREEDOM

Then Yahweh-God planted a lush garden paradise in the East,
in the Land of Delight.

GENESIS 2:8

God prepared a garden of pleasure for Adam. He placed everything good and pleasing there for Adam to enjoy. What a kind and tender Father is the Image Maker! Our perfect God placed his innocent son and daughter in a paradise in the Land of Delight. What bliss! And we will return one day to that life of paradise when the restoration of all things is complete and Christ returns.

God's intention for man is that he would be a gardener who tills the ground. Taken from the earth, he now receives the earth to till. Turning over the soil is a picture of how man must guard his heart, his life. We must become those who have been loosened and opened to the rain of God. For the tree of life must be planted and grow in the soil of the human heart! When God charged man to till the ground, it meant that he must break up the soil of his heart and prepare for the tree of life to grow in him.

The same word that means working the ground (avoda) also refers to the service and worship of God. When we think of our workplace, we must think of it as a place for God's service. This means that when we are at work, we are there to serve him in every way possible. And the Hebrew word for a "keeper" of the garden is actually the same Old Testament word for "watchman." Adam's role was to be a watchman over God's creation. He was to keep the garden and watch over it so that the serpent would not enter. Man's created role is protector, keeper—a watchman or intercessor! Intercession is built into the heart of a man. God wants to redeem this and make his men and women strong keepers and watchmen over his work on earth.

We never actually read of Adam "working" in Eden's garden. He simply walked in love with his Creator, and the garden flourished. Isn't that how we cultivate our inner life? We simply walk with our beloved, and the growth takes care of itself. Walking becomes more important than working!

What wonderful freedom God gave to man! "You may freely eat of every fruit of the garden. But you must not eat of the Tree that gives the knowledge of good and evil, for when you eat of it you will most certainly die." Everything in the Garden of Delight was for man, for his pleasure. God gave Paradise to man and woman as the love-gift of our kind, generous Father.

Is it possible that Eden was without boundaries? A river with four headwaters refreshed it. It was a land filled with gold, pearls, jewels, and abundance—yet the Bible never mentions boundaries.

It was a limitless land of freedom. The Creator gave the entire paradise of Eden to earth's first pair. It was an all-you-can-eat buffet with no fear of gaining weight. It was endless pleasure without sin. God's first command in the Garden of Eden was "freely eat" (Genesis 2:16).

Eden was radiant, and color of unsurpassed beauty filled the landscape. Its garden was a conservatory of the fairest vegetation and a storehouse of choice fruits. The only restriction was that the man and woman must continue to abide in the pleasure of God, eating only what was right and true.

God was not unkind or harsh; our God was gracious and generous to man. And he alone knows what is good for us. To enjoy the good, we must trust and obey him. He knows that true freedom was in the loving shade of Eden. He knows that if we disobey, we have decided for ourselves what is good and what is not good, and therefore, we have made ourselves a god.

The first three days of creation, it was God who called the light "day" and named the dry land "earth." Now he gives Adam the opportunity to show his likeness to the Creator by allowing him to name the living creatures. God supernaturally led the animals, perhaps two by two, to Adam to receive their names. And the animals all loved and obeyed Adam, for there was no ferocious beast before the fall. The lion was as harmless as the lamb. Man had wisdom and insight into God's work and participated with God. By naming each creature, Adam took dominion over it. When you have the power to name something, you have the power of dominion over it. This showed Adam's superiority over the animals.

The Creator placed everything under Adam's supervision. God spoke and created the universe; Adam spoke and named the animals. God assigned to man the work of one made in his image. As the living creatures came to Adam, he obviously noted that he, unlike all the others, dwelt alone without a mate. "But Adam could not find a fitting companion that corresponded to him" (v. 20).

THE GIFT OF THE BRIDE

With the original genetics of man, the Lord fashioned a companion for Adam who powerfully expanded the graces and expression of God himself. And the great gift God gave to the woman was the ability to conceive and give birth. As the two came together, mankind would express a fuller, more complete picture of God.

"It is not good for the man to be alone" (v. 18). God knew what was best for man. Man is a sociable creature meant for fellowship with others. "Two are better than one" (Ecclesiastes 4:9). Moreover, how could man bear offspring without a counterpart? The Lord provided for Adam what he needed most: a partner, a friend, a companion—literally, a "completer." We must remember that God did not just create individuals. He created community. From this marriage would come children, and from this family would come community. God made man to be in relationship with others to fulfill the purposes of God. Our need for others existed from our creation.

Every wife completes that which is lacking in the man. The Bible uses the Hebrew word for "helper" (ezer) fourteen times to describe God (Exodus 18:4; Psalm 20:2; 33:20; 46:2; 70:5; 89:19). We could never say that God is inferior to man, nor could we say that woman is inferior to man. God created man to need the help of a partner. The "image of God" is both male and female. The word "suitable" means "equal" and "adequate." The woman would be an equal and adequate partner for Adam.

Neither Adam nor Eve had earthly parents. Adam had no one to "leave" in order to bond to his wife. Eve likewise had no mother or father to say goodbye to as they joined in marriage. This shows that the husband-wife relationship is to be permanent while the parent-child relationship is temporary. Sons and daughters leave their parents to unite in matrimony. This first marriage of Adam and Eve demonstrates the primacy of the husband-wife relationship over the parent-child relationship.

Just as God created woman from man, God is creating his comparable counterpart from himself. The Spirit of Christ Jesus is producing the life of Spirit God in redeemed human beings becoming the bride of God, the Lamb's wife, the New Jerusalem (Revelation 21:9–10). God is creating a suitable companion for himself from his people on earth. The creation of mankind filled the desire in the heart of God for a counterpart with which he could produce many sons to glory. God's beautiful bride and his many sons will glorify him (Hebrews 2:10–11).

Adam and Eve are a picture of a soon-to-be-married couple: the Lord Jesus Christ (the last Adam) and his bride, the church (Ephesians 5:22–33). Jesus Christ can truly say, "I love my wife." If it is not good for man to be alone and in need of a wife, then it is not good for Jesus Christ to be alone. He longs for a bride that will complete him! Without the bride, there is something missing— something incomplete with our precious Lord. Just as a woman completes her husband, the radiant bride of Christ completes him. The Creator longs for a partner worthy to share his throne. You have become that bridal partner when you accepted Jesus into your heart!

God did not form Eve from Adam's rib but from Adam's side. Eve was not simply a "riblet" God took from an insignificant part of Adam, but God formed her from half of him. And each half, man and woman together, become the completion of the image of God. It was only after taking woman from Adam's side that God looked on his finished human creation and said, "You are beautiful," for it pleased him greatly!

Eve coming from Adam's side is a glorious picture of Jesus, the last Adam (1 Corinthians 15:45), the church, and the bride of Christ (Ephesians 5:21–33). God caused the man to fall into a deep sleep (with perhaps divine anesthesia or trance). And he formed Eve from a rib out of the side of Adam; not out of his head to rule over him, nor out of his feet to be trampled upon by him, but out of his side to be equal with him, under his arm so he could protect her, next to his heartbeat so he could love her. Adam lost a rib but gained a wonderful completion through the woman. God himself custom-built the woman for him!

The Father brought her to the man as his second self. The woman provided a brand new perspective for Adam's world. Her insights and feelings opened up for him new realms of spiritual reality. He would never be the same. For Eve, opening her eyes to see herself reflected in the Creator's eyes must have been a moment she never forgot.

The Father's intent was that the two would become one. Marriages can be made in heaven! So it was with our heavenly Bridegroom, the Lord Jesus Christ. Placed in the deep sleep of death, out of his wounded side came blood and water that cleansed and purchased the bride, bringing her to new life.

Eve was in Adam before she became the bride just as God chose us in Christ before we were born (1:4). Adam and Eve ruled together over this paradise. And the bride of Christ will rule and reign with him over a restored creation. The spiritual Bridegroom and the mystical bride are the counterparts to this story. This mystery of Christ and the church is deep indeed! Adam did not have a clue what this was all about. Yet the Son knew when the Father put Adam in a deep sleep that it was a preview of the cross and the bride-to-be that would come from his wounded side.

Adam received her and said, "Her bones were formed from my bones, and her flesh from my flesh!" This in Hebrew means more than body but also "essence" or "self." Adam was saying, "She is from my soul." Just as man was the climax of all creation, showing the honor and dignity of man, so God created the woman last. Honor is upon her as the glory of man (1 Corinthians 11:7). If the man is the head, the woman is the crown. The man was dust refined; the woman was dust doubly refined.

It appears from Matthew 19:4–6 that God himself said, "For this reason, a man leaves his father and his mother to be unselfishly attached to his wife. They become one flesh as a new family" (Genesis 2:24). A man must leave all other relationships to form a marriage and cleave to his wife. The bonds of marriage must be stronger than any other (Psalm 45:10–11). This bond or covenant is to be so secure that spouses should never weaken it by having other lovers (Malachi 2:15). Jesus also left his Father when he came down to suffer and die for our salvation. He left his mother when he was on the cross, tenderly placing her in the hands of his friend, John the beloved (John 19:25–27). Jesus left Father and mother to become one with his bride (the church).

Can you just imagine what it must have been like to enjoy fellowship with God the Father in the midst of the beautiful Garden of Eden! Nothing would hinder their relationship as part of the eternal family. Their daily walks in the cool of the day would be occasions of profound pleasure and unspeakable delight. Both

Adam and Eve were naked and unashamed in the Garden of Paradise, at ease with one another without fear of exploitation. In their nakedness, Adam and Eve walked majestically through the Garden of Delight, content to be creatures living in the comforting care of their Creator. No pride, no shame, no fear. They lived in the weightlessness of grace without experiencing the heaviness of shame. Accepted fully and accepting one another, they walked in delight and satisfaction with God and with each other. Innocence and beauty filled their days as husband and wife as they lived in perfect harmony. This was God's plan, and it will be restored on earth once again.

LET'S PRAY

My wonderful Father, I give you thanks today for who you are. I'm convinced of your great love for me. No matter what I have done, your love for me is constant and never ending. I want to bring you delight with everything I do today. Make my life a sweet offering of praise to you. There is no one who has my heart like you, my Father. I am yours, and you are mine, and I love it that way. Amen.

11

THE TEMPTATION AND FALL

Now the snake was the most cunning of all living beings that Yahweh-
God had made. He deviously asked the woman, "Did God really tell
you, 'You must not eat fruit from any tree of the garden . . . ?'"
But the woman interrupted, "—We may eat the fruit of any tree in
the garden, except the tree in the center of the garden. God told us,
'Don't eat its fruit, or even touch it, or you'll die.'"
But the snake said to her, "You certainly won't die. God knows that
the moment you eat it, your eyes will be opened and you will be
like God, knowing both good and evil."
When the woman saw that the tree produced delicious fruit,
delightful to look upon, and desirable to give one insight, she took
its fruit and ate it.
She gave some to her husband, who was with her, and he also ate it.

GENESIS 3:1–6

The matrix of the garden was an environment of unbelievable delight and love. Yet it was in this perfect place that doubt was born. God placed one restriction, only one, on humankind. It was one reasonable, wise restriction meant to preserve and protect Adam's race.

We did not make ourselves, so we are responsible to obey, to serve, and to glorify our Creator in all things. This loving Creator gave the command not to eat of the forbidden tree to emphasize the relationship man was to have with God. But man chose to be self-seeking, independent, and self-willed. Consequently, he disobeyed God and was plunged into the black night of spiritual darkness and death.

Sin is now a universal sickness, passed on to every human being as "all who are in Adam die" (1 Corinthians 15:22). As Adam fell, we fell. Adam re-lives his life in every human being until Christ comes to live through us (Galatians 2:20; Philippians 1:21).

For the first time in Scripture we meet that mysterious one, the devil or snake. His chief aim is to get between your soul and God, bringing doubt upon the ways and words of God. He seeks to replace God in the human heart, substituting his own lies for the truth. It was Adam who gave the serpent his name as an act of taking dominion over God's creation (Genesis 2:20). Adam held the power to resist and conquer the temptations the evil one threw at him. We never have an excuse for listening to the devil's lies.

"The snake was the most cunning of all living beings Yahweh-God had made" (Genesis 3:1). This snake was apparently a very beautiful creature in his pre-cursed state. Satan is called the serpent in Revelation 12:9, 14 and 20:2. Lucifer (the serpent) was the first king of the angels. As an anointed cherub, he was likely the worship leader of heaven, the "guardian cherub," according to

Ezekiel 28:14. The name Lucifer means "light-bearer or shining one." On the holy mountain of God, Lucifer had access to the presence of the Most High, walking among the fiery stones. Under this flaming cherub was an innumerable company of angelic beings. Full of wisdom and perfect in beauty, with every precious gem as his covering, Lucifer was second only to God himself.

Yet his heart was lifted up with pride. The apostle Paul describes pride as "the snare of Satan" (2 Timothy 2:26). Lucifer was determined to ascend into heaven, exalt his throne above the stars of God, and become like the Most High. This was treason and rebellion on the highest scale. It appears that one third of the angels rallied to his support (Revelation 12:3–9). Because of God's judgment, the shining Lucifer took the form of the serpent. And this vile serpent wrapped himself around the hearts of Adam and Eve.

The Hebrew word for snake (serpent) is nachash, a very elastic term in that language. It can function as a noun, a verb, or even as an adjective. When nachash functions as a noun, it means snake; when nachash serves as a verb, it means "to practice divination or deception." When nachash has the definite article attached to it (as in this verse—the snake), it means "the diviner or deceiver." When nachash serves as an adjective, its meaning is "shining" or "polished" (as in shiny). Adding the definite article to the word, ha nachash, changes the meaning to "the shining one." Elsewhere, the Bible describes angelic or divine beings as shining or luminous, at times with this very word, nachash. "The shining one" is the literal meaning of Lucifer (see Isaiah 14:12.)

Why does the tempter appear in this story? How did he get into the garden? The only possible answer is that God allowed him to enter. He came with the permission of God to tempt Adam and Eve just as he came with permission from God to test Job.

God was testing mankind to see if we would love him willingly and freely. Notice the steps that led up to the fall:

1. Adam and Eve listened to the voice of the tempter saying, "Did God really tell you?" Instead of saying "Get behind me, Satan" (like Jesus did when the serpent spoke through Peter in Matthew 11:23), Eve listened to the evil one who challenged the authority of Yahweh-Elohim. The serpent always throws doubt into our hearts, suggesting that God does not mean what he says. His word lost its proper place of authority in her life.

2. Eve added to what God had said, tampering with God's word (Proverbs 30:6). God's command was simply, "Don't eat its fruit." To this Eve added the words "or even touch it." God had said nothing about touching the fruit.

3. The serpent finally spoke the lie, "You certainly won't die." When we believe a lie of satan over the truth of God, we are bowing down to satan and making him our lord. We now treat God as a liar. This is what has happened to fallen man! Note that the serpent's lie has to do with denying God's judgment. Even today this is a battleground in the hearts of fallen human beings. Satan wants us to believe that God will never judge us for our sins (Matthew 7:13–27).

4. The devil suggested that God was withholding something good for them. He intended to shake

her confidence in God's love. "God knows that the moment you eat it, your eyes will be opened, and you will be like God, knowing both good and evil." The enemy wants to tell you that God has not grounded his plan in love but in cruelty. "How can you place confidence in someone who doesn't love you? If he loved you, why would he prohibit you from enjoying such good things! He knows that by eating this tree you will become divine!" The serpent was drawing Eve to be God's judge instead of his worshiper.

LET'S PRAY

Father of Glory, be my protector and my wrap-around shield. I need your strength each day to face every enemy that comes against me. Give me more faith. Let my confidence rest in you and in your word and not in the lies of the enemy. I place my heart in your hands today. Keep me from temptations that would move my heart into unbelief or doubt. I humble my heart before you, and I worship you alone, my King. Amen.

12

FORBIDDEN FRUIT

Immediately, their eyes were opened,
and they realized they were naked, vulnerable, and ashamed;
so they sewed fig leaves together for coverings.

GENESIS 3:7

God's grace is what keeps us strong and pure—grace alone! We all need grace to remain pure in this world of conflict. Surrounded by favor and blessings from God, we should be constant worshippers and lovers of our King. But sadly, sin marred the beginning of our human race. Ignoring the millions of blessings, Eve saw one prohibition and allowed the evil one to twist it into a doubt of God's care. Sound familiar? Satan will always tempt you to question the love of God your Father. Jesus is God who became a man to prove his love beyond a doubt. It's time for you to know and to rely upon the love of God (1 John 4:16), for this is where the serpent will strike.

A life without limit was Adam and Eve's. No boundaries but one. The loving, caring God surrounded them with beauty and glory as a continual reminder that he is good. Look at your life today. Can you see the reminders of his care and kindness toward you?

Eve looked upon the forbidden fruit, desired it, took it, ate it, and gave it to her husband. This is how sin entered the world and how sin enters our heart. We resist the will of God, we reject the Word of God, and we desert the ways of God (2:15–17).

Satan works from without to within, the reverse of God's ways with man. God always begins his work within the heart until it is manifest in a changed life. However, satan works externally, through the bodily senses and emotions of the soul until the spirit is corrupted. The serpent slowly wound his scheme around Adam and Eve until they surrendered God's government to his vile leadership. Satan directed his appeal to:

1. The cravings of sinful man (delicious fruit)

2. The lust of his eyes (delightful to look upon)

3. The boasting of what he has and does (desirable to give one insight)

The appeal of sin is rooted in the cravings of what we cannot have, what pleases the senses, and what will make us wise and admirable before others. But true spirituality is being content and thankful for what we have and living for what pleases God.

The serpent deceived Eve; Adam walked into transgression with his eyes wide open. Adam heard directly from God the command not to eat and knew the details, but Eve heard it from Adam (1 Timothy 2:14). Both ate of the forbidden fruit and were immediately plunged into spiritual darkness. By choosing the tree of knowledge over life, man mingled himself with satan. We are no longer able to express God fully or take dominion over his creation; evil has taken dominion over us.

"Immediately their eyes were opened, and they realized they were naked, vulnerable and ashamed." The Hebrew word for nakedness is actually "emptiness." Adam and Eve knew they were empty by eating of the tree. Filled with shame, they tasted spiritual death. In a moment, the crown of God's creation became powerless, terrified creatures who were aware of what they had done. Their eyes were opened to their true condition; "miserable, poor, blind, barren and naked!" (Revelation 3:17). What sad fruit from the tree of knowledge! They could clearly see evil, and now they are without the power to avoid it.

The age of innocence was over. The discovery of their nakedness led to a self-effort to cover it: "So they sewed fig leaves together for coverings" (Genesis 3:7). This is the first record of man's effort to remedy his fall by his own devices. Every effort to remedy our condition is futile (Job 31:33). We try to cover ourselves with the things of this world (wealth, pleasures, and entertainment). We will use anything we can to try to cover our real need before we seek God. The Lord wants to cover our nakedness with what he provides by the shedding of blood.

The fall of Adam and Eve injected the "self" virus into humanity. Dying to the holy, heavenly image, men and women now live in another image—the image of the snake. The "self" virus brought all kinds of spiritual sicknesses into the human family as the lights of the holy place inside of Adam and Eve grew dim.

Satan was speaking to Eve through the snake (2 Corinthians 11:3). Through deception, satan gained power over our race, and he continues using that power by deceiving us still. In the same way he deceived Eve, he tries to lead us astray from a pure and sincere devotion to Jesus, who is our life. May we not fall into that temptation but remain ever devoted to him.

Jesus, the last Adam, overcame the snake in a garden. As he prayed in Gethsemane, Jesus wrestled with satan. Sweating great drops of blood, our Lord Jesus struggled through the night in prayer. His Father heard him, and he won the victory. Just as in the Garden of Eden, man was once again asleep to what the enemy had planned.

Adam, Where Are You?

> Then Adam and his wife heard the sound of Yahweh-God passing through the garden in the breeze of the day. So, they hid among the trees concealing themselves from the face of Yahweh-God.
>
> Then Yahweh-God called Adam's name and asked, "Where are you?" (Genesis 3:8–9)

Hearing God's voice (what would that be like?) and knowing he was near, Adam and Eve hid themselves. It was the approach of a judge that put them into fright, yet it was their guilty consciences that drove them into hiding. God came down to Paradise, not in the flaming fire of his chariot with thunder and lightning, but he came as one who still sought them out in love. He came walking in the breeze of the day, not running, but walking deliberately as one slow to anger.

God manifested himself on earth to commune with man, but

all that changed. They hid from the Lord God among the trees. Before they had sinned, Adam and Eve would have run to meet their Father-Creator. But now they were fearful and hiding. Their fig leaves failed them, and they were sensing their nakedness before a holy God. Knowing they were guilty, they didn't want to stand trial but fled from justice. Satan promised them they would be like God, but here they were as criminals, trembling, anxious to escape, and prisoners to sin. This was their very first experience of shame. Since then, we live our days self-consciously. Some are conscious of how well they are doing, others of how poorly they are doing. But all of us are in love with self, looking for a place to hide. Spiritually disabled, we are bound to the things of earth instead of the heavenly things. As the memory of the Father's face slowly faded, man's spiritual energies likewise declined and went to sleep.

God spoke this startling question: "Where are you? Why aren't you at my side?" Adam was God's friend, his chosen creation, his favorite. He had done so much for Adam, but now the Lord must ask, "Where are you?" This question was not to discover what place, but what condition Adam was now in. This was not the voice of a policeman but the voice of yearning love. And he speaks that to each one of us. "Where are you?"

The Good Shepherd went after his lost sheep. God's first words to fallen man still spoke of his grace. He asked them a question to draw them out of hiding—a voice to penetrate man's conscience and lead him to conviction over his sin. When Adam first sinned, he should have gone immediately to God to beg for mercy and forgiveness. Instead he did just what millions are doing today: he ran and hid from God so that God had to come and look for him. God knew where he was hiding but wanted Adam to admit his shame. The first question God asks in the Bible, "Adam, where are you?" shows that we belong to God. He longs for us to examine our own lives, be honest with him, and come out of hiding. The first question of the New Testament is, "Where is the child who was born King of the Jews?" And the first question Jesus asks is, "What do you seek?" Our answers to these three questions hold the keys to understanding the need of our heart, our life's passion, and God's plan for our lives (see Matthew 6:33; John 1:38–39.)

This question, "Where are you?" proves that man was lost, and God had come to seek him. How kind is our God! He comes not to issue the sentence of death but to preach the gospel. God seeks sinners! It was not Adam who sought after God, but God that sought after him (Romans 3:11). What could God have seen in man to cause him to seek him out? Fallen human beings are precious to God. Hiding from God remains part of our condition.

"I was afraid." Adam had never experienced fear before this moment. Once secure in his love before the Father, he simply walked with God. But now, the prospect of meeting God brought terror. Once secure in his belovedness, Adam was never troubled with thoughts of insignificance or failure. Clothed with the sense of divine worth, he acted out of love, not of duty or addictions. So the snake reached his goal to separate man from the Image Maker.

We're still afraid to admit our sin before God and come out of our denial. If Adam had known God's love, he wouldn't have been afraid, for love's perfection drives the fear of punishment from our hearts (1 John 4:17–18). God will not only be man's Creator, but he will also become man's Savior. God has come to make himself our Hiding Place!

LET'S PRAY

I come to you my Father. I come out of place of hiding, shame, need, and pain. I come to you, beloved Father. You are the King of my heart, and you know everything there is to know about me. Deliver me from anything that would get in the way of my love relationship with you. I will not be afraid, and I will not hide from you. I come knowing your grace and mercy surround me. Keep me in your wrap-around presence today. I will be close to you. Amen.

13

FALLEN IMAGE BEARERS

Adam answered . . . "I was afraid because I was naked; so I hid."
"Who told you that you were naked?" God said. "Did you eat the
fruit of the tree that I commanded you not to eat?"
Adam pointed to the woman and said, "The woman you placed
alongside me—she gave me fruit from the tree, and I ate it."
So Yahweh-God said to the woman, "What have you done?"
The woman pointed to the snake and said, "The shining snake
tricked me, and I ate."

GENESIS 3:9–13

Adam knew that everything had changed. He could feel it.
His spirit was dark, his soul torn, and his mind confused. He was
naked. This proves that a conscience, a moral instinct, had come
to life within him. Our crippled consciences still bear witness to

the wicked and desperate condition of man. It's the still, small voice of the Creator within our hearts (1 John 3:19–20).

Adam knew he was naked even with fig leaves. This nakedness Adam felt was a moral and spiritual one. Adam, like all of us, laid the blame upon someone else and indirectly upon God himself. It seems we will blame someone, anything else, before accepting the blame of our own actions. When true conviction grips the heart, we cry out, "It is I who has sinned and done evil."

Man had lost all: his dominion, his dignity, his innocence, and his peace with God. It was all from God, but now Adam became a fallen image bearer. There he stood—a lost, guilty, ruined sinner. Instead of a broken-hearted confession, he tried to excuse himself. The full sense and impact of Adam's reply is more horrible than what appears on the surface.

First, it was not very chivalrous. When God accused him of sin, he blamed his wife. On top of that, when he blamed his wife, he really abdicated his position as head of the household, saying to God, "I simply did what the woman told me." And the woman did no better, blaming the serpent. Sin is a brat that no one is willing to own.

Eve now found herself in difficult interpersonal relations with Adam. Do you think there was ever marital harmony after that? Do you think Eve would ever let Adam forget that he blamed her before God? There is no such indication in the Bible, but I can imagine that every time there was a little argument she would say, "Do you remember what you told God? You said it was my fault." This was the beginning of marital disharmony. The battle of the sexes began in the garden. Sin brings grief and competition to the family. Only the love of Christ can heal the wounds between men and women.

From the beginning, the voice of satan has been a voice of deception, dulling our spiritual senses and lulling us into slumber. The Young's literal translation reads: "The serpent has caused me to forget." So often the enemy of our soul will rob us of the living memory of God's Word and how it has transformed us and given us life. Instead, the serpent will cause us to forget God's goodness and replace it with his lies, his cunning lies. Deception is forgetting the truth of God. Lies will replace light when we forget how wonderfully kind God is.

THE CURSE AND A PROMISE

> Yahweh-God then said to the snake: "Because you have done this, you are cursed above every wild animal, condemned above every creature of the field! You will slither on your belly and eat dust all the days of your life! And I will place great hostility between you and the woman, and between her seed and yours. He will crush your head as you crush his heel." (Genesis 3:14–15)

God now turned to the serpent, degrading the shining snake into a loathsome reptile crawling on his belly, cursed to eat dust. God had formed man from dust (v. 19; Isaiah 65:25; Micah 7:17). Every area of our life that's not surrendered to God will become food for the devil. Our uncrucified, stubborn heart becomes the devil's dining room if we don't have a constant "Yes" to God in our spirit. Withholding our life from God feeds the enemy. The only place the devil can thrive is in the carnal minds of men. Nevertheless, to dust we don't have to return. God has lifted us out of dust and seated in the heavens (1 Samuel 2:8; Isaiah 52:2; Ephesians 2:6).

The seed or "offspring of the woman" is an obvious reference to the Lord Jesus Christ. He is the true seed of spiritual life that was planted into death but now springs up to bear much fruit in his spiritual offspring. Every other human born on earth is from the seed of the man. Only Jesus, the virgin-born, can be called the seed of the woman. Jesus was "born of a woman" (Galatians 4:4). This is a remarkable prophecy of the virgin birth of our Lord Jesus (Isaiah 7:14). We are born again not by a corrupting seed but by an Incorruptible Seed, the living and abiding Word of God (1 Peter 1:23).

The seed of the serpent is the nature of the devil sown into the hearts of men. This "seed" or "offspring" would be bound to the earth, and this is what the serpent would eat. The reason why the enemy wants us to be earthly and walk in our "dust-nature" is that he feeds on it. We're his food when we bind ourselves to our old life.

The true seed of the woman bound the serpent as the "mighty man" while he was on earth (Matthew 12:29). Jesus, as the seed of the woman, bound the serpent and plundered all his wealth. In John 14:30, he told his disciples that the serpent, the "ruler of this dark world," had nothing in him. As the seed of the woman, he crushed the serpent's head on the cross and rose again in power as our life-giving Savior. Through the woman the curse came, and through the woman the Savior would come. Through the woman, Adam and Eve lost Paradise, and by the seed of woman, we regain paradise. She is now restored in dignity by means of her children (1 Timothy 2:15).

Before he banished them from the garden, God gave Adam and Eve this remarkable promise of a coming redeemer. In the Hebrew language, the "seed" of the woman is masculine singular.

"He will crush your head as you crush His heel." This is a clear prophecy of Christ on the cross. No sooner did man fall into sin than God supplied a revelation of the cross. On the cross, satan will strike his heel, but Jesus Christ will crush his head. The cross destroys the works of satan in the human spirit. It reverses devastation, and divine life comes rushing back into the heart. On the cross, Jesus paid the full payment of Adam's transgression and removed it by his sacred blood. The Goliath of hell has fallen. Nails pierced the flesh of the Son of God, but the blood of the cross was the fatal blow to satan (Colossians 2:14–15; Hebrews 2:14). This is the Protoevangelium, God's first announcement of a Savior, and presents a preview of Jesus Christ whose heel would feel the wound of the snake but who would bring a death-blow to satan by the power of his cross and resurrection (Isaiah 53:10; Colossians 2:14).

The holy seed of the woman has overthrown satan's power as he took our sins on the cross. Satan's wound can never be healed! This perpetual curse on the serpent is also a curse upon the rulers of darkness who roam the earth today. God's eternal curse is upon them, giving the Christian dominion over all of them (Psalm 91:13; Luke 10:19; Ephesians 1:19–23; 1 John 5:18). Redeemed man carries the authority of the cross and resurrection of Jesus Christ as a weapon of righteousness against the schemes of the enemy. He may bruise us, but we will ultimately pound satan to a pulp under our feet (Romans 16:20).

The parable of the sower (Matthew 13) teaches us that Christ has sown himself into our hearts as the spiritual seed of the woman. The apostle Peter says that we have been born again, not by a corrupting seed, but by a seed that was planted within us and can never be destroyed, but will live and grow inside of us forever

(1 Peter 1:23). Christ is the Living Word, the incorruptible seed. The seed of a conqueror is in you! Every Christian has this spiritual seed living in them that will grow and mature until Christ is fully expressed through the church, his body. Look again at the words of one of the stanzas of the great Christmas hymn, "Hark the Herald Angels Sing":

> Come, Desire of nations, come!
> Fix in us thy humble home:
> Rise, the woman's conquering seed,
> Bruise in us the serpent's head;
> Adam's likeness now efface,
> Stamp thine image in its place:
> Final Adam from above,
> Reinstate us in Thy love.

Let's Pray

My glorious Father, who can be compared to you? Your wisdom is beyond understanding. All your ways are right. You know my future and have gone ahead of me to prepare my way. I thank you for giving me a Savior like Jesus! He is the perfect One for me and all I need to know you. I thank you that in him I have authority over the evil one. By your strength, I will always be victorious. I love you today and every day of my life. Amen.

14

Pain Enters the World

Then God said to the woman, "I will cause your labor pains
in childbirth to be intensified; with pain, you will give birth to
children. You will desire to dominate your husband, but he will
want to dominate you."
And to Adam he said, "Because you obeyed your wife instead of
me, and you ate from the forbidden tree when I had commanded
you not to, the ground will be cursed because of you. You will eat
of it through painful toil all the days of your life. It will sprout
weeds and thorns, and you will eat the plants of the field. You will
painfully toil and sweat to produce food to eat, until your body—
taken from the ground—returns to the ground. For you are from
dust, and to dust you will return."

Genesis 3:16–19

God desires to give himself to you. That's why he made you. He first took his own nature and likeness and fashioned a creature just like him, implanted with his image and likeness, one he could love with unlimited passion. God and man are meant to enjoy each other in the warmth of mutual love. Freely and openly we can share our lives and express our hearts. This is the divine idea. You are a thoughtfully inspired image formed in his loving thoughts. You are the divine idea.

Yet today, our lives often fail to reflect God's perfect plan. Sin has marred the image of God. God's son and daughter, Adam and Eve, failed to listen to and obey God's instructions and plunged the entire human race into a spiritual darkness that only the light of Christ can remove. Sin is a reality that we must address.

PAIN IN CHILDBIRTH

To the woman, God spoke his judgment: Motherhood would involve pain and suffering. It is as though the birth of every human being reflects the pain of sin.

Sin has brought pain and death into the world. God decreed that the labor contractions of the woman will be painful. The Hebrew word for pain is 'etsev, a homophone that can also mean "creativity." God will use our painful situations to reveal and express his beautiful creativity through us. How many works of art, compositions of music, and powerful acts of kindness have come about through the "labor pains" of our sometimes troubled past? Pain can be the incubator of creativity and beauty. Some of the creative works that you will produce may come out of the most painful periods of your life.

God condemned man to exhausting labor to make a living. Fortunately, God cursed the ground and not Adam or Eve. Work was not a part of the curse, for God gave Adam responsibility for working and tending the garden before the fall (Genesis 2:15). The punishment of the woman touched her identity as a wife and mother; the punishment of man touched his identity in his activity of work and being a provider. But, because of this curse, the earth would no longer produce food without the laboring, painstaking toil of man.

The irony of the narrative is hard to miss. Because they ate what God forbid, pain entered the world. The man would produce food to eat through painful toil, and the woman would experience painful childbirth. Additionally, the ground (and all creation) now labors with painful contractions waiting for the unveiling of God's sons and daughters (Romans 8:19–21).

God cursed the ground because of Adam's sin. Plant diseases, droughts, floods, hurricanes, and other disasters that would affect food gathering—even food shortages—are all a result of man's disobedience. Before the fall, the earth was free of weeds. Weeds and thorns added to the strife as Adam's race would eat food by the sweat of his brow. "Weeds and thorns" are a sign of man's self-defeat and God's judgment (Proverbs 24:31; Isaiah 34:13; Numbers 33:55). Weeds and thorns are like the cares of this life and the deceitfulness of riches (Matthew 13:3–23). The ground (dirt) is also a picture of the flesh of man, producing only wood, hay, and straw, striving by works to please God (1 Corinthians 3:12–13; Hebrews 6:7–8).

Jesus wore the crown of thorns on his head, a picture of the curse that he took upon himself for us (John 19:2). And he sweat great drops of blood while praying in the garden to show us that he was removing our heavy yoke of bondage (Luke 22:44). The curse of God fell on the ground because of Adam's sin. The principle here is that the land absorbs the sin of a people. The land (even a nation) carries the curse of the ancestors whose sins fell upon the ground. The blood of Christ is the only thing that can break this curse.

Sorrow. Sweat. Painful toil. Dust. Death. The wages of sin. The serpent's words were such fantasy. Didn't he say, "You will be like God!"? As deep and devastating as the fall of man was, so the redeeming grace of God is deeper still! Jesus took our sorrows, sweat great drops of blood, and he was left "in the dust for dead" (Psalm 22:15) as he became a curse in our place (Galatians 3:13). Through our redemption, Jesus not only reversed the effects of the fall, but he has brought us something much better: eternal life! We have gained more through the last Adam than we lost through the first Adam. Jesus experienced all the effects of the curse. He sweat and labored in prayer and in carrying the cross, he wore a crown of thorns, and he was brought to the dust of death (Psalm 22:15). It is true that our bodies will return to dust, but Jesus has lifted us out of the dust and seated us in the heavenly realm (Ephesians 2:1–6). Death no longer has the victory over us because the resurrection of Christ is also our resurrection (Romans 6:5).

Before the fall, man lived in an earthly paradise, but now in Christ, we dwell in the heavenly realm (Ephesians 2:6). Before the fall we were innocent, but in Christ we can become the righteousness of God through our union with him, and we can experience partnership with his divine nature (2 Corinthians 5:21; 2 Peter 1:4). Adam was lord over Eden; we are heirs of all things, and "we also inherit all that He is and all that He has" (Romans 8:17). Jesus "is not ashamed or embarrassed to introduce us as His brothers and sisters" (Hebrews 2:11). We know the bliss of pardoned sin and union with Christ. Truly, where sin once abounded, grace now much more abounds!

LET'S PRAY

Lord Jesus, you are the Curse-Breaker and Deliverer of my soul! I thank you today for carrying my sin to your cross and washing me clean. Your blood is enough. I rest in the finished work of Jesus Christ my Lord! Your love has set me free, and I am forever grateful. Keep working in my heart to make me more like you. And help me as I yield my soul to you this day. Amen.

15

EVE

The man named his wife Eve—"Life-Giver,"
because she would become the mother of every human being.

GENESIS 3:20

Adam proved his faith by naming his wife Eve ("living"
or "life-giver"). He could have called her "the mother of all the
dying." Yet, faith believed the words God had spoken about the
seed of the woman. Adam received the prophecy of the cross in
his heart, and he named his wife, Eve, "life-giver." By giving her
this name, Adam sealed this covenant and confirmed the promise
of God.

Adam changed her name from "Woman" to Eve, the first of
many name changes in the Bible. The Hebrew contains a pun,
or paronomasia, with the name Eve, for her name havvah is very

similar to the word for life (khayah, or "living one"). God gave the woman an ability not just to have babies, but also to release life in a variety of expressions. Eve brought life into the structure of Adam's world. What does the Scripture tell us about a woman? She is God's chosen 'ezer (Genesis 2:18), a protector, provider, and strength for a man. Secondly, she is taken from man, equally a partner under the Lord and perfectly matched for re-union as one. Thirdly, she is the carrier of life for all humanity. A woman enfolds all three roles in one person.

Why did God not name Adam "Father of all the living"? Because that would be a title that could only belong to God. The Creator took Adam from the earth, but our Father dwells in heaven. There is an ache for a father that someone made from earth cannot fully satisfy. We must come to know our Creator as our Father.

LAMBSKIN

"Yahweh-God made garments from animal skins to clothe Adam and Eve" (Genesis 3:21). The Creator acted as their priest and provided the sacrifice to cover their sin. God had to strip away their fabricated covering and cover them with his own. Perhaps God took a lamb, hung it on a tree before their eyes, and removed its fleece to clothe this fallen pair. Their first sight of death was an innocent sacrifice killed for them. Animal skins . . . it's as though the Father was saying that man's nature is closer to an animal's than to God. The fall marred the beautiful image he gave them. Wearing the skin of a beast reveals man's heart as beast-like. The mark of the beast came on Adam and Eve in the garden.

In the form of a tree, the tree of life, God offered himself to man as food, food that would bring them life. But man refused and fell into sin so that once again God provided a covering in the form of a Lamb. As Adam rested in the Lamb as his clothing, his covering, he could still live. God the Father revealed the first drop of blood man saw providing their salvation. By this illustration, God taught Adam and Eve about the cross, salvation, and the need for a substitute. Mercy sought to spare the sinner, but justice required an innocent substitute. God taught them what salvation would require and what it would impart.

God covered Adam with a coat of the lambskin, and he became one with the lamb. The sinner became one with the substitute. This is union. Substitution has nothing to do with us until we enter that union. Once we participate in union, whatever the substitute has accomplished is ours.

The robe God provided was adequate; the fig leaves Adam used were not. God's righteousness will cover man's sin, while man's righteousness is always sin-stained and inadequate (Isaiah 28:20; 64:6; Zechariah 3:3–5; Luke 15:22–23). When Adam stood clothed with God's garments, he couldn't say he was naked. There were no more excuses to hide from God while wearing the garments of righteousness.

Clothed in lambskin, Adam and Eve looked like lambs. Although he was a man, Adam had become a lamb in the eyes of God because we're covered in Christ, the Lamb of God, and we share his righteousness (Galatians 3:27). Now we resemble and express him. The sinner becomes one with the Substitute. Even the clothing God made for Adam preached the gospel. One day you will meet Adam and Eve in heaven! It's time for you to know the what to wear. Do you possess this seamless robe (Revelation 3:18; Isaiah 61:10)?

EXPULSION FROM EDEN

> And Yahweh-God said, "The man has become like one of us, knowing good and evil. And now he might take in his hands fruit from the tree of life, and eat it, and live forever." Therefore, Yahweh-God expelled him from Eden's paradise to till the ground from which he was taken. (Genesis 3:22–23)

Adam and Eve had only known the presence of their Father and Creator. They'd never lived a day without his comforting presence surrounding them. Now they were banished from their source of joy and comfort.

It was imperative that God did not allow man to eat of the tree of life, or he would live forever in his present condition. Man must taste the tree of life only in resurrection (Revelation 2:7; 22:2). To live forever in a body of sin and death would be intolerable for God's purpose with man. God wants man to live in Christ, not in his sins (John 5:14).

God covered their faces with shame so that they would seek him (Psalm 83:16). And he drove man out—and kept him out (Job 18:18). The continual memory of what we once had is still etched deeply into our spirits. We don't know exactly how to define it, yet we feel it. The lonely ache in our soul is real. Pleasure is hollow without God as its source. Relationships are still unfulfilling without the living presence of God within. We've all been there. We've known the emptiness, a distant memory somewhere in our soul of a time when we came out of the breath of the Almighty.

LET'S PRAY

God, you have made me for yourself. From nothing to something I have come to be. I offer you my life, my identity, my future, my plans, and my heart. I forever long to be yours. Give me a heart that pursues you even when I am discouraged or weary. Give me a passionate love for you, my Creator, that endures for the rest of my days. I want to make your dream come true. I love you, my God. Amen.

16

THE CHERUBIM

He drove them out of the garden, and placed fearsome angelic
sentries east of the Garden of Eden, with a turning fiery sword to
guard the way to the tree of life.

GENESIS 3:24

Have you ever seen an angel? I have. They are incredible
beings. But these angelic sentries were nothing to mess with.
I don't think I'd want to encounter one of those! God stationed
cherubim with flaming swords to guard the tree from man. Nevertheless, the Lord Jesus Christ opened "a new and living way"
into the paradise of God, the Holiest of Holies (Hebrews 10:20;
John 14:6). Jesus restores Eden and opens the veil for man back
into paradise. The last Adam had to leave a garden too so that he
might bear the sins of the world (Mark 14:46).

The text says that God "placed" fearsome angelic sentries at the garden gate. However, the Hebrew word for "placed" is the word from which we get "Shekinah." You could almost say, "God Shekinahed" with angelic sentries at the garden gate. It is possible to translate the last verse of this chapter, "And he (God) dwelt at the east of the Garden of Eden between the cherubim, as a shekinah (a fire-tongue, or fire sword) to keep open the way to the tree of life." The inference here is that God "tabernacled" at the entrance to the garden in the flames of the cherubim—his mercy seat!

We usually read this passage as though God has barred man from the tree forever and that there's no way to get back to it. But that's not true. There is a way to return to this tree. It's not a physical way but a spiritual way named Jesus Christ. "I am the way, the truth, and the life." These were the words of the one who once walked with Adam and Eve in the breeze of the day in his temple-garden.

The fearsome angelic sentries held a fiery sword. This is the first reference to a sword in the Bible. We know from Hebrews 4:12 that the sword is a picture of Word of God as it judges the secret motives of the heart. We still must pass through the ministry of the "flaming sword" to get back into the place where God desires that we dwell. This sword was "awakened" against the Lord Jesus Christ as he paid the full price to redeem us to God (Zechariah 13:7). Because the Shepherd was smitten, we, the sheep, are spared!

THRONE BEARERS OF GOD

Nowadays man has shrunk the cherubim down and fashioned them into little chubby babies with fluttering wings. We use them as adornments on statues, sit them prettily in our gardens, and etch them into the sides of our buildings. However, cherubim are not tiny little angels but are large and magnificent. The Hebrew masculine word for cherubim was kerub, translated as "one who intercedes" or "knowledge," borrowed from the Assyrian language from a root word meaning "to be near." The Bible mentions cherubim four times. In Psalm 18:9–10, David describes the sudden descent of Yahweh to rescue a soul in distress in the following words:

> He stretched open heaven's curtain
> and came to my defense.
> Swiftly he rode to earth
> as the stormy sky was lowered.
> He rode a chariot of thunderclouds amidst
> thick darkness,
> a cherub his steed,
> soaring on outstretched winds of Spirit-wind!

Scripture also describes cherubim as God's charioteers. The Hebrew word kerub has been associated with the Hebrew word rakab, "to ride," and merkeba, "a chariot." The Bible often uses these two words interchangeably. One of the functions of the cherubim is that of throne bearers, or "carriers," of his divine majesty, hence their depiction as charioteers.

The words "Who sits upon the cherubim" or "Who dwells above the cherubim" or "Who is enthroned above the cherubim" (depending on which version of text you are reading) are frequently found in the Bible (1 Samuel 4:4; 2 Samuel 6:2; 2 Kings 19:15; 1 Chronicles 13:6; Psalm 99:1; 80:1; Isaiah 37:16). This refers to Yahweh's actual dwelling in the Holy of Holies with the cherubim surrounding him and refers to them as the heavenly throne bearers of God.

Genesis 3:24 depicts the role of cherubim as guardian spirits, but they were also present in the ark of the covenant, covering the mercy seat (Exodus 25:18–22), wrought in massive gold. According to 1 Kings 6:23–30, Solomon placed in the Holy of Holies two huge cherubim of olive wood overlaid with gold. They most likely faced the holy place or the entrance.

In Exodus 26:31, God instructed his people to embroider cherubim on the veil of the tabernacle that separates the Holy Place from the Holy of Holies. "With blue, purple, scarlet and fine twisted linen they were made." How many they embroidered on the veil, we're not sure, but we do know that their presence depicts guardian spirits or keepers as the veil screened the Holy of Holies.

Besides here in Genesis 3:24, the next place that we see cherubim in Bible is in connection with atonement, showing mankind the only ground on which creation could hope for the end of its groaning. This is where we read of cherubim embroidered on the veil and engraved above the golden mercy seat. And in 1 Kings 6–7, Solomon engraved cherubim as an artistic motif in wood and metal. He covered the paneling of the temple, both interior and exterior, with them as well as palm trees and flowers. And he adorned the molten sea with figures of lions, oxen, and cherubim.

Fallout

So Adam and Eve vacated the premises. They left behind the Garden of Delight. They tasted the depths of woe in a bite. They had mistrusted God and embraced satan. Their sinful choice flung sin's door wide open and shut the gate to the beautiful garden of

God! Man now began his emigration from God and lost the light that once burned bright. With a broken heart and a guilty conscience, Adam and Eve began a different life outside of Eden's gateway.

Man not only lost the garden, but he also lost the glorified presence of God. But thanks be to the triumph of Jesus Christ, for he has torn the veil of separation from top to bottom, providing us access to his mercy throne. God's desire is and has always been that man would enjoy him as the tree of life, but his glory (the cherubim), his holiness (the slaying sword), and his righteousness (the flaming fire) kept fallen man away. No one can get through these three. If man is ever to eat of the tree of life, he must fulfill the requirements of God's glory, holiness, and righteousness.

Note the seven results of the fall of humanity and how Jesus is the answer:

1. The ground was cursed, but Christ was made a curse for us.

2. Sorrow and tears are part of our lives, but Christ became the man of sorrows.

3. Sweat is a part of the curse, but Christ sweat drops of blood.

4. Weeds and thorns now grow on the earth, but Christ wore a crown of thorns.

5. Suffering and death entered earth, but Jesus suffered and died for us.

6. A sword kept man from God, but the way to God is now open by the pierced side of Christ.

7. Man was separated from God, but Jesus took away that separation.

My friend, are you living in the full access that Jesus has given, or are you just standing at the open gate? Through Christ, the cherubim with the flaming sword have stepped aside. The veil is torn, and sinners have access to the Holy of Holies. Are you accessing what the Image Maker has provided for you? Are you stepping inside his realm and seeing and enjoying the grace gifts that Jesus has given to you?

What are some of the signs that you're not accessing all that is available to you today?

- You still see yourself as naked, vulnerable to hurt, accusation, and shame.

- You try to hide and have an instinctive reaction of feeling guilty.

- You blame-shift: It's someone else's fault.

- You point your finger at God, blaming him.

- You're still finding that life is difficult, painful, and burdensome, while yearning after freedom.

God drove man out of the garden so that he might bring us back. The God who pursued Adam after his fall will pursue him still. The Creator kept the tree of life from man for a time so that man might have it for eternity. We are now living in the age of the open gate. Christ has re-opened the garden gate for all who will come. Jesus extends an invitation to eat from the tree of life.

Let's Pray

Father-God, you are the God of abundance. You have given me abundant life in Christ. Help me to eat the fruit of the tree of life that grows in me. I long to taste the delicious fruit of Christ's fullness each day. Fill me with longings for you, cravings that can only be satisfied by feasting upon you. Thank you for full and complete access to all that you are and all that you have. I love you, God! Amen.

17

AM I MY BROTHER'S SHEPHERD?

But with Cain and his offering, Yahweh was not pleased.

GENESIS 4:5

In Chapter 3 of Genesis, we saw the beginning of sin in mankind. Now in Genesis 4, we see the beginning of sin in the family. Sin is a contaminating leprosy, spreading death in its wake. In Genesis 3, sin was against God, but in the next chapter, it's against man. When we lose the fear of God, we will not respect our fellow man. How devastating is the poison of sin!

Adam and Eve had many sons and daughters (5:4), but Cain and Abel seem to have been the two eldest. Some even believe they were twins. Eve said after the birth of her firstborn, Cain, "By the grace of Yahweh I have birthed a man" (4:1).

Many Hebrew scholars believe a more accurate translation would read, "I have brought forth a man—Jehovah" (the God-man).[11] This implies that Eve believed the promise of her "seed" (3:15) and presumed that Cain would be the promised one. What a disappointment when Cain became a murderer!

Imagine the hope and anticipation Adam and Eve had for their firstborn. They had never seen life given that way before. This was the first baby born in the world. It was a marvelous, miraculous experience. Think of all the wonders of childbirth and what happens when we have our first babies. We would have painted the nursery blue. We would have dreamed about all the great things this baby would accomplish. But, instead of being the Christ, he was a killer.

The second son born to Adam and Eve was Abel. His name means "vanity" or "fading away." Perhaps this is because their hope for the Messiah had faded. Or maybe they saw from the weeds, the thorns, and the hard ground that life was much more difficult outside the garden than inside, so their joy faded away. Paul tells us in Romans 8 that the world was made subject to vanity. Adam and Eve saw this vanity first-hand and named their son Abel.

Their first son, Cain, was a farmer, and Abel was a shepherd. Cain "became a farmer, working the ground." He was bound to the earth from which he had been taken. He did not realize or receive the heavenly life. Since he was a farmer, Cain thought that he could offer the fruit of the ground to God. In bringing the offering of the product of the cursed earth, Cain was denying that he was a guilty sinner, insisting on approaching God based on personal worthiness.

Abel was a shepherd. Before the flood, people did not use sheep for food (Genesis 1:29) but only for sacrifice. Abel had his heart set on the coming sacrifice. He brought the first and best of his flock as a sacrifice in faith. By so doing, Abel acknowledged that he was worthy of death and that God required a substitute. He presented his offering "by faith" (Hebrews 11:4).

Cain and Abel both presented their offerings to Yahweh. In verse 16 we read, "And Cain left the presence of Yahweh" (Genesis 4:16). That seems to indicate there was a specific place where God dwelt. It could very well be that the Shekinah glory was suspended there over a mercy seat where the cherubim stood guard and where they would go at various times to offer their sacrifices.

"Yahweh was very pleased with Abel and accepted his offering, but with Cain and his offering, Yahweh was not pleased" (vv. 4–5). The attitude of Abel's heart was right, making his sacrifice acceptable. But Cain's was not right, and thus he brought a polluted offering. Worship is a matter of the heart. God did not just care about the correct offering alone but also the attitude of the heart. God detests the sacrifice of the wicked and finds it despicable "when people use the worship of the Almighty as a cloak for their sin" (Proverbs 15:8). God did not accept Cain's bloodless offering. Sin's guilt must be removed.

You can almost see the offering Cain brought . . . a big fruit buffet. How beautiful with its pineapples and apples and figs and other delights! It was certainly more colorful than a meat buffet. When you look at a bloody pot roast next to oranges and bananas and apples and grapes, there is no comparison. But Cain's sacrifice did not involve the shedding of blood, and only the shedding of blood can cleanse sin's stain.

It was not that God did not want the fruit. Later in Leviticus 19:24, God will say, "Bring the fruit." The problem is that Cain had it out of sequence. Before we can bring the fruit, we must have forgiveness and new life. First, the blood that brings the forgiveness of sins and then the fruit of praise and good works. Cain wanted to bring the praise without forgiveness. So, God had no respect for Cain's offering. He did have respect for Abel's offering. For Abel's bloodstained sacrifice signified:

- He believed the report of his parents. God had killed a lamb and covered them with its skin.

- His sin required the death of an innocent one to cover his guilt before God. Abel, by faith, knew that he could approach God through a sacrifice. This is why in Matthew 23:35 he is called "righteous Abel."

Cain and Abel take us back to the true worship of God and the false worship of God. Here we follow to their fountainhead the two streams that empty themselves in heaven and into hell. They are the saved and the lost. And the dividing line between them is a line of blood.

Abel is a clear type of Jesus Christ who, as a Shepherd, brought the sacrifice of himself to God and was killed by his jealous brethren (John 15:25; Matthew 27:18). God called Abel's offering "a more acceptable sacrifice" (Hebrews 11:4), and Abel was therefore "declared righteous." Cain he was just as righteous as Abel. It wasn't necessarily that Abel was better, but his sacrifice was. How do we know that God accepted Abel's sacrifice? Perhaps fire fell from heaven to consume his offering.

Since Cain was a tiller of the ground and Abel was a tender of sheep, it is likely they had already offered blood sacrifices to God at the gateway to Eden. Cain would have had to purchase his sacrificial lamb from his younger brother Abel. It's possible that every time Cain bought a lamb from his brother, Abel would say,

"Isn't this great that God gives us a way to cleanse our sin and to go into his presence?" As the months and years wore on, it's likely that Cain, who had allowed the evil one in, began to chafe under the need to continually go to his brother for a sacrifice.

Cain began to rebel as his father Adam had. He began to hate God's prescribed method for coming into his presence. His pride began to well up, and it became too much for him. He had lost faith. After all, he was the number one son, and through him the blessings were supposed to come. Now he had lost that right.

As Cain saw himself passed over while Yahweh blessed his brother, his heart filled with rage. Cain was furious that all his labors counted for nothing. So he rejected the Lord's counsel and became angry over his brother's approved sacrifice. If Cain had presented his offering in the right spirit, there would not have been anger in his heart when he realized God had not accepted it. Instead, he would have had a humble, teachable heart, willing to learn the ways of God and to accept the opportunity to change.

But Cain never asked God, "What is wrong? Lord, what can I change?" He was merely angry and jealous. Therefore, Cain turned away from presenting a blood-sacrifice and instead relied on his own reasoning and vain conceit. "Claiming to be wise," he became a shallow fool (Romans 1:22). God had ordained the way for his people to approach him, but Cain chose the way of self-will.

As Cain saw God accept Abel's sacrifice, he reasoned that his little brother would now rule over him. This is what angered him the most. So he decided he would rather kill his brother than to have his brother rule him. This is the real motive and the cause of the first murder in history—jealousy! Brother Cain just could not stand the thought of God blessing someone else over him!

Let's Pray

Father God, I honor you and reverence you. I bow in deepest adoration before you. No one could ever take your place in my heart. May my sacrifice of praise be lifted up into your heart today. Free me from any influence that would hinder my worship of you, the living God. Deliver me from the temptation of jealousy. Let me rejoice when I see my brother or sister blessed. I want to reflect your glory in all things. Thank you, my God! Amen.

18

Acceptable Worship

So Yahweh said to Cain: "Why are you so angry and bothered? If you offer what is right, won't you be accepted? But if you refuse to offer what is right, sin, the predator, is crouching in wait outside the door of your heart. It desires to have you, yet you must be its master."

Genesis 4:6–7

Jealousy and violence are an issue of worship. Cain wanted to worship God his own way. And he became angry when he could not. So many today insist on bringing to the Lord the worship that they believe is right instead of what God truly desires. The Lord was giving Cain the opportunity to humble himself and be glad over his brother's accepted sacrifice. In doing so, Cain could have received exaltation and learned how to rule over sin. If Cain had been glad in his heart that God respected his brother's sacrifice, he would have gained what all of us are looking for: elevation, exaltation, and dignity.

This is not only the way to receive elevation and honor; it's also the way to rule over sin. If we can rejoice over others receiving honor, even when it's over and above us—when our offering is inferior to theirs—we have learned how to rule over sin.

God was clearly telling Cain that if he would offer the right sacrifice, he could regain the rights of the first-born. The real difference between Cain and Abel was in their sacrifice, for God would have cleansed even Cain if he had done what was right.

"If you offer what is right, won't you be accepted?" God is speaking about offering the right sacrifice, a blood sacrifice, not the fruit of the cursed earth. The Hebrew translation is "Will you not have the excellency?" or "Will you not be exalted?" This refers to the rights and privileges of the firstborn. For only by bringing an acceptable sacrifice would Cain qualify to rule over his brother.

A literal translation of the verse is "If you do well, uplifting?" Scholars consider this verse to be one of the more difficult verses in Genesis to translate. The implication is that God would lift up Cain with favor (forgiveness) and accept him if Cain did well by bringing an acceptable offering. This is not condemnation but an invitation for Cain to change his ways. The Hebrew word "uplifting" comes from the root word nasa', which means "to carry away, to take away, to lift up, to bear (iniquity), to forgive." Abel's works were righteous, and Cain's works were evil (1 John 3:12).

However, at the same time, God solemnly warned Cain of a greater sin "crouching in wait" outside, desiring to have him. The ancient Aramaic translation reads, "Your evil lord awaits you at the gate of sin."

Here we see a word picture of sin, like a lion crouching in the shadows to maul Cain. The Hebrew word for door is "opening" (as in "the door of his conscience" or "the opening or gate of his soul"). Or it could translate to "crouching, resting outside the portal." The Akkadian word for crouching (rabisu) is frequently associated with a demon. The image of sin is as a demon-beast crouching at the door of Cain's heart. However, the word for sin can also mean "sin-offering." God could have been telling Cain that there was a sin-offering, as a resting lamb, lying outside his door to be the acceptable sacrifice. If the sacrifice was acceptable, the portal (in Hebrew, patach) to God's presence would open. Both sin and Jesus are knocking on our heart's door waiting to come in (Revelation 3:20).

The serpent talked Eve into her sin, but not even God could talk Cain out of his. God told Cain, "Yet you must be its master." Sin is always the fault of man. We do not sin accidentally. God tells us that we have the responsibility to master sin. But how do we master it? By offering a faith sacrifice, by trusting in the blood of the innocent substitute, The Lamb of God. His cross is the key to victory over sin. He is the Master who mastered sin by his sinless life and his sacrificial death. We master sin when we yield to the life of the Master, the one who mastered sin in every dimension.

THE FIRST MURDER

One day Cain said to his brother, "Let's go out into the field." When they arrived at the field, Cain rose and attacked and killed his brother Abel.

Then Yahweh said to Cain, "Where is your brother Abel?"

He answered, "How do I know? Am I my brother's keeper?" (Genesis 4:8–9)

"One day Cain said to his brother . . . ." The verb "said" has an unusual use here. It is a rare Hebrew word used only in some of the old cognate languages. Other literature uses the word to mean "making an arrangement for a meeting." If that is the translation here, then it is saying that Cain arranged for a meeting with Abel. So whatever Cain was going to do, it was premeditated. He made arrangements for a meeting out in the field, far from any possible interference. He already knew what he was going to do. It was first-degree, premeditated murder.

As they walked toward this remote area, Abel, whom the New Testament calls a prophet, was probably exhorting and encouraging his brother regarding what God had said to him. "Cain, you need to submit yourself to God and get rid of that prideful spirit. Go back. I'll sell you a lamb; I'll give you a lamb. Offer it to God, and he'll be satisfied and accept you." So, as Abel is preaching to his brother in the field, Cain slays him.

The very first death in the Bible was the death of a martyr who died because of his faith. Cain's act of murder was the devastating consequence of false worship and religious jealousy. In 1 John 3:12 we learn that "Cain . . . yielded to the evil one." And why did he murder Abel? "Because his own actions were evil and his brother's actions were righteous." There is nothing worse than religious jealousy. This is what caused the death of our Lord Jesus Christ. The religious system could not understand how God could approve of Jesus over them.

Oh, the darkness of sin! Cain killed his own brother, a good brother who had done nothing wrong. In killing his brother, Cain struck out at God, for it was God's acceptance of Abel that gave birth to the envy filling his heart. Cain hated Abel because God loved him. Yet how many times do we speak evil or hold malice in our hearts toward one of our own brethren in Christ. To hate a brother is the sin that Cain committed (Matthew 5:21–22; 1 John 3:15).

We must always keep in mind that when there were just two brothers in the whole earth, they could not get along—one murdered the other! Problems among the brothers are a part of this fallen planet, and sadly, a part of church life. Even so, the Lord will release even greater measures of love to his sons and daughters that will empower them to lay down their lives in love for one another. The world has yet to see the church filled with the measureless love of Christ.

On the way back from the murder scene, God stopped Cain in his tracks asking, "Where is your brother Abel?" Cain's self-centered reply was, "How do I know? Am I my brother's keeper?" This is a statement of sarcasm, for it could rightly be translated, "I don't know. Shall I shepherd the shepherd!" Cain rejected responsibility for his sin. God gave Cain a chance to repent by asking, "Where is your brother Abel?"

The Creator sought to draw out a confession, but Cain pleaded not guilty, adding rebellion to his sin. He covered a deliberate murder with a deliberate lie; "How do I know?" But how can one hide sin from God? Cain was insolent, blurting out, "Am I my brother's keeper?" Not, "Am I my brother's murderer?"

We speak the language of Cain when we neglect to show concern for the hungry, the destitute, the broken, and the defenseless (Philippians 2:4). Although everyone is responsible for his or her own actions, we cannot turn away from one in need (1 John 3:17–18). We are our brothers' keepers. We are to guard our souls and to guard the lives and souls of others. To protect and serve is the motto of the police department in your city. It would be a great motto for our lives too.

LET'S PRAY

Lord, I want to be a helper and a keeper of others. Make me a person whom others would want to connect to, and make me a person who will easily connect to the heart of others. I want to live outside of myself for your glory. Help me to help others every way that I can. Open my eyes today to see how I help and serve my family, my church, my community, and the nation you have placed me in. Flow through my life today as I serve your kingdom purposes. Amen.

19

THE CRY OF BLOOD

Yahweh said, "Listen—the voice of your brother's blood is crying out to me from the ground! What have you done? Now you are banished from the land, from the very ground that drank your brother's blood from your hand! [12] *When you try to cultivate the ground it will no longer produce crops for you; and you will be a fugitive, a homeless wanderer!"*

GENESIS 4:10–12

Innocent blood cried out for justice from the ground. God spoke as if Abel's blood were both a witness and a prosecutor. The most important words in this sentence are "to me." The blood cries out to God, and he hears it. Blood has a voice!

The Hebrew translation is "The voice of your brother's bloods, drops of blood." Blood crying is a symbol of the soul crying out for the right to live, demanding the punishment of the murderer. Bloodguilt calls for justice, even from the ground. It is as if the face of the earth blushes as it becomes stained by blood. Blood (spilled) outside the body is always plural in Hebrew, "your brother's bloods." This speaks of his descendants that could have lived. Their blood too cried out against Cain. The blood of Abel cried out for vengeance. But the blood of Christ cries out for mercy and pardon. Therefore, the blood of Christ speaks a better word than the blood of Abel (Hebrews 12:24).

Abel is a type or picture of Jesus Christ:

- Abel was a shepherd. The Lord Jesus is the Good Shepherd (John 10), the chief Shepherd (1 Peter 5:4), and the great Shepherd (Hebrews 13:20). "The Lord is my best friend and my shepherd" (Psalm 23:1).

- Abel's brother hated him without a cause. We read in John 15:25 that Jesus's brethren hated him.

- Cain slew Abel because of envy. Cain was envious because his brother found acceptance in the sight of God and he did not. Matthew 27:18 says that his enemies delivered up the Lord Jesus because of bitter jealousy.

- Abel did not die a natural death but a violent death at wicked hands. Acts 2:23 says Jesus died by lawless hands.

- Abel died according to the flesh, and so did Jesus Christ (v. 36).

- The blood of Abel still speaks (Hebrews 11:4); the blood of Jesus still speaks (12:24).

THE MARK OF CAIN

> Cain said to Yahweh, "My punishment is more than
> I can bear! Look—you've thrown me off the land today,
> and now I must hide from your presence. As a fugitive
> and wanderer on the earth, anyone who meets me may
> choose to kill me!"
>
> Yahweh responded, "Not so! If anyone kills you,
> I promise the seven-fold vengeance of Cain will be
> released upon him!" So, Yahweh put an identifying sign
> on Cain as a warning so that no one would dare kill him.
>
> Then Cain left the presence of Yahweh and journeyed
> to the Land of Wandering, east of Eden. (Genesis 4:13–16)

Cain complained of the sentence God passed upon him. He didn't acknowledge the greatness of his sin, only the greatness of his punishment (Lamentations 3:39). He saw himself exposed to the hatred and ill-will of all mankind. Wherever he wandered, his life would be in danger. Unpardoned guilt fills the heart of man with unspeakable terrors (Proverbs 28:1; Job 15:20–35; Psalm 53:4–5). Cain's complaint was that his punishment did not meet the crime. He stated it was too much for him to bear. The Septuagint translation of this verse reads, "Is my sin too great to be forgiven?" The Hebrew word 'avon means "sin and its punishment." The Hebrew translation of this verse can mean "my sin" or "my punishment" is too great to bear.

The Lord took both sustenance and shelter from Cain. As a wanderer, he would spend his days with a stained and condemning conscience. He would remain a fugitive and a vagabond all the days of his life as he carried an "identifying sign," the mark of Cain. It could have been a visible mark upon Cain as a warning that he was under divine protection (Ezekiel 9:4, 6). However, it is also possible that God showed a supernatural, authenticating sign to confirm to Cain that no one would harm him. Ancient rabbis taught that the mark of Cain was a horn that grew on his head.

This mark or sign was both a mark of rejection and a mark of protection. Cain was cursed, separated to evil, and under the wrath of God. We all deserve this curse, and it is only in the grace of Christ that we inherit a blessing instead (Galatians 3:10, 13). Every fallen human being carries the mark of Cain—rejection.

Every one of Cain's race knew that deep inside, they were not acceptable. Fear of rejection and the fear of man are the fruits of sin. Fear brings insecurity, leaving us all with façades of independence and self-sufficiency to protect us from rejection. Only the blood of Christ and the love of our Bridegroom-King can remove these fears from the heart. In his love we become secure.

Cain journeyed on to the "land of Wandering," or "the land of Nod," the Hebrew word for "wandering." It was likely a symbolic place. There was a span of 130 years from the creation of Adam to the murder of Abel, which would have allowed for other sons and daughters of Adam to spread over the earth. Some have calculated there could have been over a half million people alive at that time (Genesis 4:25; 5:3). Scripture does not mention the line of Cain after this chapter, nor does it mention Cain's death.

God decrees, "killing Cain costs seven lives"[13] (Genesis 4:24). If someone had killed Cain immediately, no one would remember him. But by preserving his life, God made Cain a monument of justice. The mark of Cain would distinguish him forever as the man who killed his brother. The Lord then banished Cain from his holy presence to the Land of Nod. Cain renounced God, leaving the presence of the Lord for a life of futile wandering.

THE STEPS OF CAIN

Notice what the Bible says about "the steps of Cain" mentioned in Jude 11. They are:

1. The way of human reason

2. The way of unconfessed sin

3. The way of jealousy

4. The way of anger and strife with a brother

5. The way of self-righteousness and striving

6. The way of murder

7. The way of condemnation

8. The way of despair

9. The way of wandering

LET'S PRAY

Lord, my wandering heart has found a home in you. I am so thankful for the rest and the peace you give me. Your forgiveness is my shelter and my hiding place. When I have failed you, I come to rest in your love and know that you have forgiven me. Help me to stay close at your side in the days to come. I trust in you, my Lord and my God! Amen.

20

THE DESCENDANTS OF CAIN

Cain slept with his wife and she conceived and bore Enoch. Cain was building a city at the time, so he named it the Village of Enoch, after his son.

GENESIS 4:17

This early civilization, which perished in the judgment of the flood, was somewhat advanced. Cities grew along with the development of the arts and manufacturing. The descendants of Cain took the lead in producing cities, music, weapons, and agricultural implements—civilization itself. "The wickedness of humanity deliberately smothered the truth and kept people from acknowledging the truth about God" (Romans 1:18). This is the way of the world as humanity copes with life under the curse of sin (Psalm 17:14; 127:1). Man produces a culture without God.

God sentenced Cain to a life of wandering. Capital punishment would be a lesson of justice that God would teach man after the flood, but for now, Cain received a life sentence and, out of rebellion, he built a city where he could permanently locate in defiance of the Most High.

It is God's intention for mankind to live in a city. This is God's dream for his people, a city called the New Jerusalem and a people called the bride of Christ. This bridal-city will one day be the dwelling place of both God and men, the city whose builder and architect is God. But it will not come until man is ready to live in it with God. In our arrogance, we go about building cities without God and assuming we are able to live together without the grace and presence of Christ. Our imposing cities and technical brilliance are dim shadows compared to the light of the coming city, the New Jerusalem people who will shine bright as the sun.

The fugitive formed a family. In the Jewish tradition, some believe that Cain, of necessity, married one of his sisters (Genesis 5:4), who gave birth to Enoch. By naming the city after his son, Enoch, Cain attempted to retain the memory of his descendants (Psalm 49:10–11).

The line of Cain continues with Enoch, Irad, Mehujael, Methushael, and Lamech.

Here are the names of the sons of Cain and the sons of Seth (Genesis 4–5):

The Line of Cain	The Line of Seth
Adam	Adam
Cain	Seth
Enoch	Enosh
Irad	Kenan
Mehujael	Mahalalel
Methushael	Jared
Lamech	Enoch
Jabal	Methuselah
Jubal	Lamech
Tubal-Cain	Noah
Naamah	Shem, Ham, Japheth

Here are the meanings of the names of the line of Cain:

The Line of Cain

Name	Meaning
Adam	man
Cain	selfishness
Enoch	teaches
Irad	fugitive
Mehujael	blotted out by God or God is combating
Methushael	they died who are of God
Lamech	overcomer, powerful, one who brings low

When you put these names together in a sentence, this is what we find: Man is selfish and teaches us that when we become a fugitive from God's presence, God will combat us until we are blotted out by him in judgment. Many good people suffer persecution, and they died who are of God. Even when evil men are powerful and seek to be overcomers, God will bring them low!

Now notice the meaning of the names of Seth's line:

The Line of Seth

Name	Meaning
Adam	man
Seth	appointed
Enosh	pain or suffering
Kenan	to die
Mahalalel	the splendor of God
Jared	come down
Enoch	teaches, instructs
Methuselah	his death will bring
Lamech	powerful, overthrower
Noah	rest

When you put the names of the descendants of Seth together, this is what we find: The descendants of Seth show that man is appointed to pain and suffering and to die. But the splendor of God, Jesus Christ, has come down to teach us that his death will bring into our lives the powerful overcomer who will lead us all into rest!

It's amazing what hidden messages we can find in the genealogies!

LAMECH

Lamech married two women, Dawn and Dusk. Dawn
gave birth to Jabal, the first of those who lived in tents
and raised livestock. Jabal's brother was Jubal, the first of
musicians who played instruments. [14] Dusk gave birth to
Tubalcain, the first of blacksmiths who forged all kinds
of bronze and iron tools. His sister was Naamah.

Lamech boasted to his wives:
"Listen to me, Dawn and Dusk!
Mark my words, O wives of Lamech!
I have killed a man for wounding me,
and a young man for bruising me.
If killing Cain costs seven lives,
for Lamech, it will cost seventy-seven! (4:19–24)

Lamech, the descendant of Cain, was a bloody and barbarous
man who took two wives. He corrupted God's ideal of marriage as
stated in the garden. He became a man of violence and vengeance.
The names of his wives were Adah ("dawn") and Zillah ("dusk" or
"shadow"). His second wife was only a shadow of a wife, for when-
ever we turn from the righteous plan of God, we take to ourselves
only a shadow of what could be. The sons of Lamech and Adah
were Jabal (a man who raised livestock, which suggests wealth)
and Jubal (a name meaning "musician" or "jubilee").

The children of Lamech and Zillah were Tubal-Cain ("a smith
or metallurgist"—the inventor of weaponry) and a daughter
Naamah ("the lovely one"). These became the wealthy, the artisans,
and the musicians—the beautiful people of their day, who walked
in the vain spirit of the world and produced a culture without God.

Then we find Lamech singing a chorus of threats and warning. He was the ultimate warrior and used the instruments of iron made by his son, Tubal-Cain. As he strutted in front of his wives, he boasted of what would happen if someone hurt him. This was a violent, angry taunt to others to leave him alone. He added to the sin of Cain with this vow of violence and was willing to take an even greater curse than that of Cain.

Do you see the progression here? God told Cain that anyone who injured him would receive a sevenfold retribution (v. 15). This is what Lamech referred to. He was saying, "If God would avenge Cain seven times, then I am the type of person who will avenge seventy-seven times." Lamech was a boastful, arrogant, angry reviler of men. We see him telling his wives that killing others will be his business. With a seared conscience he became the world's first terrorist.

Let's Pray

Almighty God, I want nothing to do with anger, jealousy, and violence. Make me a peacemaker, one who walks in your ways, moment by moment. Deliver me from every form of anger and fear. Let my words be pleasing to you. I want only to be close to you. I love you, my God! Amen.

21

THE LINE OF SETH

*Adam slept with his wife again and she bore a son whom she
named Seth, meaning "appointed," for she declared, "God has
appointed for me another son to replace Abel, because Cain killed
him." After many years Seth had a son named Enosh. During his
lifetime, people began to worship Yahweh and pray to him.*

GENESIS 4:25-26

I'll never forget the birth of our three children. Each was
special, and each new arrival to our family changed us forever.
Children truly are a blessing from God.

Eve gave birth to another son, who was prophetically named
Seth. Seth means "appointed" or "new beginning." Apparently,
Adam and Eve realized that God would appoint this son to replace
Abel and follow on in the ways of God. This was an act of faith for

Adam and Eve. This child renewed their hopes. Seth fathered a son whom he named Enosh ("mortal" or "frail"). After the birth of Seth and Enosh, "men began to call on the Name of the Lord." Seth realized that human life was weak, frail, and mortal. This is the commencement of corporate worship.

The word "Lord" is Yahweh, the name of the God who is personal, the covenant-keeping God that man can know. The Hebrew states, "Men began to call on the Name Yahweh." To call upon the name of the Yahweh is a biblical description of prayer that includes praise and worship. The name Yahweh expresses his personality ("He Who Is and Causes to Be") and reveals his desire to commune with human beings. And worship of God among men began. This was the first revival/awakening in the Bible! For calling on the name of the Lord implies prayer, worship, and intercession. They stirred themselves to seek God, not only in private but also in public assemblies.

It is the name of the Lord, the revelation of who he is, which draws the heart of every human being to worship. His name is the true center of spiritual fellowship and intimacy. Divine revelations from Yahweh maintained and encouraged this worship; for wherever two or more are gathered in his name, he will be in their midst (Matthew 18:20). It is always the heart of God to meet with his worshipping people and to manifest himself through his presence.

We know that prophetic ministry began with the prophecies given by Enoch (Jude 14–15). The prophet Enoch foretold of the Second Coming of Jesus Christ. God told Adam and Eve about the first coming (Genesis 3:15, 21). But it was Enoch, the seventh from Adam, who received even more revelation as he prophesied of the return of Christ.

Enoch also prophesied about the flood by naming his son Methuselah. One translation of the name Methuselah is "his death will bring the flood."[15] It was the year Methuselah died that the flood came. Do you see why Methuselah lived so long? God was giving mercy to the sons of Adam to repent!

From a single pair in Eden, within seven generations, the human family would have grown to considerable dimensions. At the birth of Seth, Adam was 130 years old and had many sons and daughters whose names the Bible does not mention (Genesis 5:3–4). Over time, Cain's posterity between creation and the flood would be great enough to populate cities. Some have estimated that the population of the earth at the time of Lamech was around one million. Civilization without God is chaos—chaos as great as Genesis chapter one.

GENESIS 5

Genesis 5 is a remarkable chapter. It is the "written account of Adam's line." The history of man begins with death and pain but will one day end with delight and pleasure as the redeemed become the dwelling place of God. The destiny of God's people is to become the New Jerusalem company who will live forever at his side.

God created male and female and then blessed them. Throughout Genesis, God is the one who loves to bless his people. He called this newly created couple "man,"[16] or Adam. We can make no stronger statement that male and female are co-equal before their creator.

There's really only one who represents man in the Old Testament, and that's Adam. There is only one who represents man in the New Testament, and that's Jesus. Two men represent the human race—the first Adam and the last Adam, Jesus Christ. The books of Genesis and Matthew both begin with the record of the generations of Adam and Christ.

We notice the obituary of Adam: "The lifespan of Adam was 930 years and then he died" (5:5). God's man had now tasted death. Imagine how startling it was to the generations of his family as they saw the first God-formed man dead and gone! Adam's son, Seth, was 800 years old at the time. Adam's grandson, Enosh, was 695 years old when his grandfather passed away. Enoch was 308, and Methuselah was 243.

Genesis 5 is a description of the reign of death that came into the human family by sin. It's the litany of the death of the human race. It's filled with names that are difficult to pronounce, with the number of years each one lived, with the repeated words "and then he died." Death has passed upon all men (Romans 5:12).

God created us in his likeness, but Adam's descendants were born "in his own likeness." The poison of sin passed to all generations. Adam passed his moral likeness to his offspring. Seth was begotten in the likeness of a sinful father. Nothing that man does can change this death sentence. Man is lost and helpless because of sin. The works of man cannot shake off this dominion of death. Only when we are begotten again in Christ does he finally lift the death sentence from us.

Notice that Adam and his descendants all lived over 800 years, some over 900 years. God prolonged their lives to show his mercy and to speedily populate the earth. Many of those whose names are on the list in Genesis 5 were able to meet with Adam and hear his own account of the fall, the story of God providing the coats of skins, of casting them from the garden, and the promise of a redeemer.

We can see an interesting comparison between Genesis 5 and Matthew 1. Genesis is the book of death, and Matthew is the Lamb's Book of Life. The entire Bible centers on these two books: the book of the generations of Adam and the book of the generations of Jesus Christ. We can thank God that our names are written in the Book of Life as part of the generations of Jesus Christ!

LET'S PRAY

Lord Jesus, thank you for including me in the family of God. Your life and your Spirit have made me one with you. I'm moved deeply by knowing that you have received me as your dear child. Fill me with love and grace and truth. I want to represent you, my Image Maker, in every way. I give you my heart today. Amen.

22

ENOCH AND METHUSELAH

When Enoch was 65, he fathered Methuselah. Enoch walked with
God for 300 years after Methuselah was born and had many other
sons and daughters. Enoch and God walked together as intimate
friends; then God took him to himself, and he was seen no more.
The lifespan of Enoch was 365 years.
When Methuselah was 187, he fathered Lamech. Methuselah lived
an additional 782 years after Lamech was born and had many
other sons and daughters. The lifespan of Methuselah was 969
years, and then he died.

GENESIS 5:21–27

The story of Enoch is fascinating. He was born 622 years after
God created Adam and heard Adam tell the stories of God walking in the garden and speaking with Adam and Eve in the cool of

the day. Perhaps Enoch's desire for intimacy with God came from hearing these incredible accounts. Enoch was the one taught of the Lord as he walked in the Spirit. Here are some of the things we can learn about Enoch's life:

- Enoch's name means "dedicated, instructed, or experienced." His name speaks of his character and the revelation he carried.

- Enoch was a remarkable man of faith and righteousness. He is one of but two men who walked with God and went to heaven without passing through the gates of death.

- He was a man who pleased God (Hebrews 11:5) even though the days in which he lived were wicked and godless. The corruption of man was filling the earth, but he stood faithful in a prophetic ministry.

- Enoch walked with God in friendship and fellowship, a man of faith and purity, for God won't be found walking with those who hide their sin (1 John 1:6–10). But a holy God walked with a sinful man—what grace! To walk with God means we cease walking in our own ways to follow his. It implies Enoch surrendered his will (Amos 3:3) with no controversy between him and God. A steady walk with God for hundreds of years!

So, how did Enoch please God? Hebrews 11:5–6 supplies the answer: Enoch was a man of faith. To walk together with someone means you must like him. Enoch liked God and enjoyed the sweet communion of walking in the sacred garden with him. They communed one with the other. They enjoyed one another. And Enoch loved to be in the presence of God.

As God's friend, Enoch grew in the prophetic anointing and in friendship with the Creator. Enoch's life was not a monastic life full of isolated piety. He was a happily married man with sons and daughters. He walked with God while living a normal family life. For three hundred years, they walked as divine friends. Finally, God said, "Enoch, you have walked with me long enough. Now let me take you to myself. Instead of going back home to your house tonight, how about just coming home to my house."

Enoch was a prophet under the instruction of the Holy Spirit. He walked in the spirit of wisdom and revelation (Ephesians 1:16–17). He walked with God in a prophetic lifestyle, with a sanctified reputation and in spiritual communion with God. And he prophesied about the return of Jesus Christ thousands of years before Christ was born. Enoch is the first prophet mentioned in the Bible (Jude 14–15). As a preacher of righteousness, he predicted the judgment of the Lord. Many of his spiritual experiences were recorded in the three "Books of Enoch." Many of the early church fathers respected his writings. He wrote of such subjects as angels, which he referred to as "watchers." Jude 14–15 quotes one of the passages he wrote. It describes him exhorting the people of his day to reform their evil ways. The "Book of Jubilees" relates that Enoch was carried into paradise where he writes down the judgment of all men. Ancient Arabic legend declares him to be the inventor of arithmetic and writing.

Enoch was taken away when he was caught up into heaven without seeing death. He was the exception to the rule of death. After reading six times, "and then he died," the seventh time we read, "God took him away." Because he didn't live like the rest, he didn't die like the rest. God took him because he delighted in him (Hebrews 11:5). He lived a year for each day of the year: 365

years. God took him to give us as an example of a man who had fulfilled his destiny. God carried him across to the other side. He was walking with God one moment on earth by faith and the next in heaven! Faith turned to sight; faith became perfect fellowship (Revelation 3:4).

God took him is a Hebrew word (laqach) that can also mean "God took him in marriage," as a man takes a bride in marriage. Luke included Enoch in the genealogy of the Son of God (Luke 3:23–38). He was a man who walked in faith and was translated from earth to heaven without dying (apotheosis).

There must have been a tremendous manhunt for Enoch. Relatives must have said, "Where did God take him?" Enoch's wife would have asked, "Why?" God took Enoch to be with himself to show that death was not the end; there is a better place to go. Both Enoch and Elijah did not face death. Elijah was taken up into heaven by a whirlwind. Perhaps the whirlwind of Ezekiel was the escalator that took Enoch into the presence of God.

There was another Enoch mentioned here in Genesis—Enoch, a son of Cain (Genesis 4:17). The first city in the Bible was named after this Enoch. Not too many of us have a city built in our name! These two Enochs were contemporaries. No doubt, Enoch, the son of Cain, was voted most likely to succeed in the eyes of the world. He would be the one who others would never forget. However, it was Enoch, the son of Jared, who goes down in history as the one who walked with God so closely that he disappeared into the glory realm. Which is more important to you, to have a city named after you or to walk with God?

Methuselah, Enoch's son, was the longest living man in the Bible. For 969 years, God warned the world about coming judgment. God has been warning us even longer than that, for we have had the New Testament for two thousand years.

Jewish writers say that Methuselah, Noah's grandfather, died seven days before the flood, and that Noah and his family entered the ark the day Methuselah died (7:10). Methuselah's life overlapped Adam's by 243 years. I wonder what conversations Adam and Methuselah might have had.

LET'S PRAY

Jesus, I want to walk so close to you that Enoch gets jealous. I want to be so close to you that I feel your heartbeat and know your innermost thoughts. I want to walk in union with you. Take me into yourself. Show me the revelation secrets that you reveal to your lovers. I come close to you, closer than ever before, until I experience daily life-union with you! Amen.

23

NOAH AND THE NEPHILIM

When Lamech was 182, he fathered a son and named him Noah,
saying, "He will relieve us from our hard work and painful toil,
and from the ground that Yahweh cursed." Lamech lived an
additional 595 years after Noah was born and had many other
sons and daughters. The lifespan of Lamech was 777 years, and
then he died. After Noah had lived 500 years, he fathered Shem,
Ham, and Japheth.

GENESIS 5:28–32

Noah, the great-grandson of Enoch, had a word of prophecy over him when he was born. His father, Lamech, prophesied, "He will comfort us." Lamech was obviously a man of faith that believed God's promise and warning through the prophet Enoch.

Life under the curse was difficult and toilsome, but God had a plan for Noah.

The Hebrew name Noah means "rest," and it sounds like the Hebrew word comfort. This was a prophecy that Noah would become a type of Christ in his building of an ark and in giving comfort to the human race. The fulfillment of this prophecy would be comfort to the cursed earth. Noah brought comfort, but the one that Noah typifies brings us true rest. "Are you weary, carrying a heavy burden? Then come to me. I will refresh your life for I am your oasis . . . You will find rest and refreshment in me" (Matthew 11:28–29).

Noah was the tenth generation from Adam. Ten is the biblical number of trial and human responsibility (i.e. ten words/Commandments, Exodus 20:1; Daniel 1:12; Revelation 2:10). There are ten more generations between Noah and Abraham.

There is a sense in which Noah becomes the second father of the human race. Noah and his sons repopulated the earth after the flood. The names of his sons were Shem, Ham, and Japheth. Shem was the father of the Semitic (Abrahamic/Jewish people). Shem means "fame." It's the line of Shem from which Jesus was born. Ham was the father of the dark races whose descendants inhabited the torrid regions. His name means "hot" or "dark." Japheth was the father of the Caucasian races. His name means "spreading forth."

THE "NEPHILIM"

When people began to populate the earth, they had many lovely daughters. Divine beings found them very appealing, so they took the women they wanted as their wives. Yahweh said, "My Spirit will not strive with humanity indefinitely, for they are mortal. Their lifespan will be shortened to only 120 years." Back then, and later, there were giants on the earth, who were born as a result of the unholy union of heavenly beings with the human daughters. They were the mighty ones of old, warriors of renown. (Genesis 6:1–4)

These verses have been the subject of debate for centuries. Many scholars consider it to be the most difficult passage in Genesis to interpret. The passage raises this question: Who are the "divine beings" (or "sons of God") in verse two? Are they angels or the godly line of Seth that intermingled with the Cainite women? Most of the early church fathers interpreted "sons of God" to mean angels that fell from heaven and had sexual relations with the daughters of men (Job 1:6; 38:7). The Syriac version and the Septuagint (a Greek translation of the Hebrew) reads "the angels of God." This presents a puzzling scenario. Fallen angels having sex with women?

There is much debate over the identity of these divine beings, yet we see that they are linked to the Nephilim (giants), the corrupting of the divine "seed of the woman" (Genesis 3:16) who was to come and the judgment of God through the flood. Many scholars view "the sons of the gods" as sons of Seth. However, there is no evidence that the line of Seth is a godly line. In fact, only Noah was righteous in God's eyes. Other scholars see the Nephilim as a reference to a group of fallen angels who, in rebellion, "went outside their rightful domain of authority and abandoned their appointed realms" to have sexual relations with women. Consequently, they were "bound in everlasting chains . . . in the dark abyss of the underworld" (Jude 6). The argument that they could not be fallen angels because angels cannot marry (Matthew 22:30) is in reference to angels who are in heaven, not the angels who came to earth as part of satan's plan to cohabitate with women and corrupt the human race. Virtually all the earliest writings of Jewish and Christian literature interpret the phrase "the sons of the gods" as heavenly beings known as fallen angels ("watchers").[17]

Second Peter 2:4–5 speaks of these fallen angels in the context of God's judgment of the world in the days of Noah. The activity of these demonic powers with the daughters of men grieved God's heart and moved him to destroy the world. Satan was seeking to corrupt the "seed of the woman" that would come forth to crush him as satan would bruise his heel (Genesis 3:15). Satan sought to destroy the human race by producing a race of monstrosities.

The warning God gives man is that he will have an end of his patience. "His Spirit will not strive with humanity indefinitely" against the perversity of the human heart (6:3). The word "strive" in Hebrew means "made low." God warns, "My Spirit will not always be made low in man," or "My Spirit, the Divine breath, shall not be put low in man forever." It is supposed by some scholars that Genesis 6:3 is a quotation from one of Enoch's prophesies contained in the Book of Enoch (Jude 14–15).

Numbers 13:33 recounts that the spies which Israel sent into the promised land were dismayed and felt as small as grasshoppers at the sight of the sons of Anak, whom the verse states are in the linage of the Nephilim. Second Samuel 21:16–22 (repeated in 1 Chronicles 20:4–8) mentions the last five giants in the Bible. David and his mighty men killed four sons of a fifth giant residing in Gath.

There are only two ways to kill giants in the Bible. Intimidation never works when you are facing a giant (Numbers 13–14). Like David, we must prophesy their downfall, run straight toward them, knock them down, and cut off their heads (1 Samuel 17:48–51). Like Caleb and Joshua, we must conquer them and see them as "bread" to strengthen us. David also raised up giant killers among his mighty men (2 Samuel 21:18–22; 1 Chronicles 20:4–8).

God created man to be in fellowship with his Creator. Now we see man deserting his best friend to slide even deeper into darkness. Sin provokes God; it grieves his holiness, challenging the Maker to judge mankind (Isaiah 63:10). God saw the fountain of sin in the human heart. Every inclination, every motivation, every effort in the heart of man at that time was toward promoting evil from morning to night. How offensive is sin to God!

Yet what mercy he has shown us! It is the spirit of mercy that lives inside our hearts today, giving us grace to live in the Spirit of Christ and not the spirit of this age. What does it do to you to know that God's heart is filled with pain when we sin against him? Sin damages a relationship with the one who loves us. We violate trust, we ignore his love, and we trample on his grace each time we sin. God does not merely see our sin like a distant judge but also as an offended friend (Isaiah 43:24; Ezekiel 6:9). Sin wounds his heart. Who would want to wound the heart of a loving God?

LET'S PRAY

Father in heaven, I bow before you this day in awe of your great love and mercy toward me. I offer my life to you as a living sacrifice. I never want to wound your heart or stray from your path. May your Holy Spirit guide me into paths of righteousness for your great name's sake. Help me discover the hidden source of supernatural life in Christ that dwells in me. By faith, I lay hold of eternal life this day. I will live in your sweet presence no matter what happens around me today. I love you, my God! Amen.

24

NOAH'S ARK

But one man found grace in the sight of Yahweh, Noah.

Noah was the first man to be born after Adam died. And he was the first man to seek out the grace of God and to lay hold of it. He sought grace, for grace is the foundation of every life that pleases God. It was the grace of God, not the virtue of Noah, that preserved Noah from the devastation of judgment. This is the first mention of grace in the Bible. It's interesting that we see grace at the climax of man's sin. This clearly shows us that there is nothing within man that would merit the grace of God.

It was grace that preserved Noah in those days of incredible wickedness. It enabled him to set his face against the whole current of public opinion and conduct. Yet notice Noah's response to this grace God showed to him:

- "Noah completed all these preparations and did everything exactly as God had commanded him" (Genesis 6:22).

- "Noah obeyed all that Yahweh had commanded him" (7:5).

- "Two of each animal . . . entered the ark with Noah as God commanded" (vv. 8–9).

- "Both male and female went inside as God had commanded Noah; and Yahweh himself shut them in" (v. 16).

Four times Genesis tells us that Noah did all that God commanded him. Grace leads to obedience, not independence or waywardness (Philippians 2:12–13). Noah was a solitary and lonely figure because he was the only one who found favor with God in that terrible, terrible time. The Bible says he was a godly man of integrity, without fault in his generation.

Noah was living in the time that God was about to release his judgment to destroy the earth, but God provided grace to escape that judgment, and Noah was the one who found it.

No one escapes divine judgment except by God's grace. Genesis doesn't say Noah found grace in the eyes of men but in the eyes of Yahweh. Even though there were "warriors of renown," God had a servant in the land, a true giant of the faith.

God looked for a man who would save mankind, and that man was Noah. When God comes down, he comes down in human vessels and brings us deliverance and salvation. Noah was a perfect illustration of this: God wanted an ark, but first he looked for a man with a heart for him to build it. He desired a partner to be his hands on the earth.

NOAH'S FAITH

Noah was a godly man of integrity, without fault in his generation, a man who lived close to God. A godly man of integrity means that he was righteous and accepted based on sacrifice, covenant, and faith. We too are made righteous by faith (Romans 5:1). This is why the great faith chapter (Hebrews 11) includes Noah in the list of fifteen believers. Most importantly, Noah walked in fellowship with God. It's only as we walk with God that we avoid the evil of our age.

Hebrews 11:7 tells us a lot about Noah: "Faith opened Noah's heart to receive revelation and warnings from God about what was coming, even things that had never been seen. But he stepped out in reverent obedience to God and built an ark that would save him and his family. By his faith the world was condemned, but Noah received God's gift of righteousness that comes by believing."

We can see how vividly this passage defines Noah's faith:

- The basis of his faith – God's word, "warnings" by God.

- The extent of his faith – His heart received "things that had never been seen."

- The virtue of his faith – He built the ark "in reverent obedience to God."

- The evidence of his faith – He "built an ark to that would save him and his family."

- The witness of his faith – "By faith the world was condemned."

- The reward of his faith – Noah "received God's gift of righteousness that comes by believing."

In contrast to Noah, the earth was corrupt and filled with violence: God . . . saw how debased the world had become, for everyone was corrupt to the core (Genesis 6:11–12).

There was senseless violence, corruption, and wickedness, and demonic offspring were roaming the earth. So the Lord God was moved to destroy the earth. God spoke to Noah, warned him of the flood, and gave him a means of escape. How do you suppose God spoke to him? Did he come in human form? Perhaps he appeared in a burning bush or as an angel or in a dream? God speaks in whatever way he chooses, and he likes to speak to those whose ways are blameless. And so, Noah moved with faith and acted on the revelation given to him. Do you respond when God speaks?

In verses 14–22, we read the details for the building of the ark and Noah's obedience to God's commands. Noah's ark clearly represents the Lord Jesus Christ. Just as Noah's ark delivered his family from the flood, so Jesus delivers those who believe in him from the wrath of God. Jesus is our ark!

Here are comparisons of the ark to Jesus:

- Noah made the ark of cypress wood, which, in Scripture, often represents the humanity of our Lord Jesus.

- The ark had only one door, and we have only one savior (John 10:9; 14:6).

- God instructed Noah to set the door in the side of the ark, and Jesus was pierced in his side (19:34).

- The ark had three levels, and Jesus provides salvation for body, soul, and spirit (1 Thessalonians 5:23).

- There was a window in the ark providing light into the third loft, and Jesus is the one that provides us with light (Psalm 27:1).

- There were many rooms (nests) in the ark, and our "Father's house has many dwellings" (John 14:2).

- Noah coated the ark inside and out with pitch, which is a symbol of the "atonement,"[18] and the blood of Christ atones for sin and delivers us from judgment.

- The ark endured the fury of the flood, and Christ endured the wrath of God for us (Psalm 42:7).

- The ark was God's provision for Noah, and Christ is God's provision for sinners.

The arks of the Bible each speak of the Word of God: Noah's ark, Moses's ark, and God's ark of the covenant. The Hebrew word for ark is tevah, which can also mean "letter" (that is, words). Noah and his family, as well as the animals, survived as a result of obeying the "letter" of the Word of God and entering the Tevah-Ark. Likewise, our hope of salvation is found in hearing and obeying the Word of God and his will. We find safety and shelter in the place where God has established his Kingship and Kingdom rule: Yeshua, the Living Word, our Ark.

Let's Pray

Lord Jesus, Yeshua my King, I come to you, the Living Word of God. I am so grateful that you have given me the Word as a light to my path. You are my Ark of Glory that saved me and rescued me. Your grace has brought me salvation. I want to say that you are wonderful, glorious, and mighty, and I bow before you this day. Amen.

25

GOD THE JUDGE

So, God said to Noah,
"I have decided that all living creatures must die."
GENESIS 6:13

We must always remember that God was long-suffering with man before he determined to destroy the earth. God waited mercifully. For almost a thousand years, God was long-suffering with man, waiting for him to repent and walk with him. Mercy postponed judgment. "During the time of Noah, God patiently waited while the ark was being prepared" (1 Peter 3:20).

Just in case you might feel that God made a mistake when he judged the earth, note the revelation that he gave to the people of the world before judgment day came:

- God revealed his truth through the created world (Romans 1:19–20).

- God gave the people the promise of a Redeemer (Genesis 3:15).

- God taught them of blood sacrifice through the "coats of skins" and Abel's offering.

- The "mark of Cain" on his forehead was a continual reminder of judgment.

- They had the prophecy of Enoch, the birth of Methuselah, and the strange disappearance of Enoch.

- They heard the preaching of Noah and saw the building of the ark (2 Peter 2:25).

- They had the ministry of the Holy Spirit striving with their hearts (Genesis 6:3).

God's people despised and rejected his divine revelation. And in spite of what God revealed, they deliberately persisted in wickedness. They had no excuse. And with their sins stacked up to the heavens, God determined to wipe out the inhabitants of the earth by a worldwide flood. This judgment would cleanse the earth of its wickedness and give Noah a fresh start. God said to Noah, "But as for you, I will establish my covenant of friendship" (verse 18).

God gave a solemn promise to Noah, guaranteeing his preservation and security. And this covenant convinced Noah that God would keep his word. For God had given him instructions regarding the animals coming two by two into the ark and instructions regarding the necessary food to preserve them. He had told Noah ahead of time what was going to happen.

Consider how Noah must have felt knowing that the end of

the age was upon him. For 120 years, he faithfully preached without affirmation, applause, or approval from anyone on earth. He saw the dreadful wrath of God coming to the earth, and his ears heard the terrifying cries of an entire civilization coming to their doom. What a burden he carried. How did he process the catastrophic destruction of all those outside the ark?

In Ezekiel 14:14, God lists Noah with Daniel and Job as an overcomer. These were men who stood fast against all opposition. Daniel stood in opposition of a king, leaders, and roaring lions. And Job stood fast in the face of physical oppression, the loss of his family and his wealth, along with great emotional pressure. Like them, Noah moved in reverent obedience in building the ark (Hebrews 11:7).

This was a heroic act of faith as Noah endured the scorn and pity of the ungodly. According to Jewish traditions, the flood arrived 1,656 years after the creation of Adam. By calculating the dates of these events, scholars conclude that Noah's sons were born twenty years after God gave him the instructions for the ark.

Ark of Refuge

Noah's ark was not a prison but a refuge and a hiding place from the storm of judgment, just as the Lord Jesus Christ is our Ark of Refuge. And the Lord is ready to receive all those who come to him.

Just as God saw Noah as a "godly man of integrity," so he knows those who belong to him. Yes, he knows those who keep themselves pure in times of wickedness, and he will keep them safe in times of judgment.

At creation, God placed all the animals under the dominion of man (Genesis 1:26). God now gave Noah the charge of taking the animals, male and female, into the preserving confines of the ark. He led seven pairs of every kind of "clean" animal and two of every kind of "unclean" animal into the ark, all in seven days' time. Noah and his family were to use the clean animals for sacrifices and food after they left the ark. Some calculate that the ark had room for over seven thousand species of animals.

While Cain built a city, Noah built an ark. When the time came for the animals to be supernaturally drawn to the ark, God drew them by his power. He brought a multitude of animals to the door of the ark in only seven days. What a miracle! Only God could subdue the beasts of the earth and cause them to enter the confines of this floating zoo. It must have been quite an amazing site for the unbelievers of his day to witness hundreds of animals streaming into Noah's neighborhood, providing a visible conclusion to the sermon Noah had preached for 120 years. We wonder why his neighbors didn't join Noah inside this ark of safety when they saw this miracle taking place before their very eyes!

During these seven days, there was no sign of rain or storm and so no reason to suspect that judgment was imminent except for Noah's words. Yet Noah moved with holy obedience and prepared the animals to ride out the storm. He moved by faith when the warning of God was spoken.

THE FLOOD

It started in the six hundredth year of Noah's life, in the second month on the seventeenth day. On that day, all the fountains of the subterranean deep cracked open, and burst up through the ground. Heaven's floodgates were opened, and heavy rains fell on the earth for forty days and forty nights. (Genesis 7:11–12)

The aged Noah had served God faithfully, so as the waters burst forth to cleanse the earth of its wickedness, Noah and his sons and their wives were spared. Some historians calculate that this would have been either October or November. God had waited until Noah and his family could gather in the produce of the earth so that the animals and their caretakers had enough food stored up to sustain them. Truly, the ark became a "laboratory of mercy and kindness" as Noah spent his waking hours in the floating zoo caring for the animals (Proverbs 12:10).

"Heaven's floodgates were opened." And from beneath the surface, giant fissures burst open with massive amounts of subterranean waters. "The ocean depths he poured into vast reservoirs" (Psalm 33:7). These reservoirs, or "storehouses," sprang up and flooded the earth.

At creation, God had fixed a "boundary line," setting "doors and bars in place" that the waters could not pass (Job 38:8–11; Psalm 104:9). At the time of the flood, he simply removed those restraints, and the waters gushed forth to flood the earth as they had done at first (Genesis 1:9). This was a true cloudburst (Job 26:8, 37:11). For forty days and forty nights without stopping, the awesome judgments of God poured out upon all the earth. He made the earth in six days and took forty to destroy it! It's impossible to escape the righteous judgments of God when we resist his warnings (20:27). It's time to trust and obey God's word as Noah did. For it is the Father's heart that we might all be saved!

LET'S PRAY

Father, I know you are for me, not against me. I know that your love is greater than any circumstance I encounter today. I praise you that Jesus, my Sin-Bearer, took the judgment that I deserve. I thank you that I will forever be with you, for I believe in your Son, Jesus Christ my Savior. We will be one forever. Thank you, my God! Amen.

26

AND THE WATERS ROSE

Yahweh himself shut them in.

GENESIS 7:16

Have you ever felt like the Lord has shut you in to a place you didn't understand, a place that doesn't make sense, yet you can't escape? For some, waiting in that shut-in-place is unbearable. God shut Noah and his family and the animals in something like a box. Have you felt "boxed in" lately?

There are times when God confines you and boxes you into a situation you would never choose. But if you could see into his heart, you would see that he's doing it to preserve you and to lift you up. It's in a place of confinement, in that "box," that God can prepare you for promotion and power. God will use those boxed-in places to take you to the next level.

It was Yahweh who shut the door (Genesis 7:16) to secure Noah from the waters of judgment and to keep out those who believed too late. For at least seven days, the door of the ark stood open. All could have come in if they had forsaken their sin and believed.

What terror must have seized their hearts as they realized that old Noah was right and that they were wrong. Judgment surrounded them, and they had no place to hide. When God shut the door, no one could open it. Very soon, God will again shut the door of mercy for all humanity. Now is the time to warn others, for the time will come when they will knock and the door will not open to them!

What horrors await those who reject the mercy of God! The Father holds open the door, but they have a choice. Many will choose to drown in their lusts, sensuality, and vice until they face the judgment of Almighty God (Proverbs 1:24–25).

"The waters rose over twenty-two feet above the highest mountains" (Genesis 7:20). Water covered the earth to a depth of over three miles! The mountains crumbled and the hills disappeared, but God's covenant of peace with Noah remained (Isaiah 54:10). Who was it that measured the waters out in his hand? Who was it that knew the water covered the mountains more than twenty feet? Not Noah—he couldn't get out of the ark to measure it. It was God. Never did death triumph like it did on this day. The flood came and took them all away (Matthew 24:19).

"Every living thing on the earth perished" (Genesis 7:21). The universal flood destroyed all the unbelieving. But God is just in all his works. He who made man as he pleases may destroy man as he pleases. Who are we to question the mighty works of God?

God did what was right. The earth was corrupt, and its inhabitants were thwarting the plan of God. There needed to be a new beginning.

Pause and ponder this tremendous judgment. Can we now see and say, "It is the most terrifying thing of all to come under the judgment of the Living God!" (Hebrews 10:31). Who can stand before his anger? Who can quench judgment fires when his holiness is provoked?

"Only Noah was left behind, and those who were in the ark with him" (Genesis 7:23). Thousands fell at his right hand, ten thousand at his left, but Noah lived. Mercy triumphed over judgment. The saving grace of God prevailed for Noah's household. "When sudden storms of life overwhelm, you'll be kept safe" (Psalm 32:6). Only Noah remained. Even the godly Noah delivered only himself and his family (Ezekiel 14:14). Righteousness delivers from death (Proverbs 10:2; 11:6). Truly, Noah found favor in the eyes of the Lord.

"God's heart was moved with compassion as he remembered Noah" (Genesis 8:1). How faithful and merciful is God to Noah! To say that God remembered Noah is not to imply that God had ever forgotten him. God's heart returned to the one who found favor with him (Luke 1:72). God was about to fulfill all his promises to Noah. The fury of God's wrath against sinful man subsided, and mercy rose in the heart of Elohim. God did not forget Noah (Isaiah 49:15–16). In wrath, God remembered mercy (Habakkuk 3:2).

God commanded the wind to blow causing the waters to recede (Psalm 148:8). Perhaps this was the same wind that God sent to part the waters of the Red Sea (Exodus 14:21). He sealed up the springs of the deep and closed the floodgates of heaven. God alone holds the keys. For 150 days the waters had flooded the earth, and now it was time to dry it up. The waters had baptized the world in judgment, but now the sun would kiss the earth again.

We're so quick to view this Bible passage as merely a story of judgment, but it contains a greater theme: the saving grace of God. Certainly, death and destruction prevailed at the time of the flood, but so does mercy. In every act of God's judgment, there's always mercy.

The ark rested on the "seventeenth day of the seventh month" (Genesis 8:4). The commandment the Lord gave at the institution of the Feast of Passover changed the seventh month to the first month for Israel. Passover was the fourteenth day of the month. Three days later would be the seventeenth day of the month, the very day Jesus rose from the dead. The final resting place of our ark of salvation was the top of the mountain. Jesus was raised on high, seated at the right hand of the Most High!

So, Noah opened the window of the ark and released a raven while the waters receded. And the unclean bird flew back and forth and likely fed on the floating carcasses of men and beasts. Then Noah sent out a dove that promptly returned, signifying that there was still no dry land to be found. After seven days he released the dove once more, and it returned with an olive leaf in its beak, proving to Noah that the trees had begun to appear. Then after another seven days, he released the dove, and it didn't return, telling Noah that the land had finally dried up.

The raven and the dove reflect the two natures of the believer. The raven was an unclean animal representing the fallen, corrupt nature of every person. It feeds on death and decay and on the things that pertain to our flesh and mortality (Romans 8:6). The carnal mind will rest on anything except Christ.

The symbolism of the dove is that of the Holy Spirit. The three outgoings of the dove from the ark are symbolic of the work of the Holy Spirit in human history. The first time Noah sent the dove out, it fluttered over the dirty waters, but having no place to rest, it returned to the ark. So, in the ages before Jesus, the Holy Spirit went throughout all of humanity but didn't find a resting place. He touched men here and there, but he didn't abide with them. The Holy Spirit couldn't build a nest in the hearts of men, so he returned to the heart of the Father.

The second time the dove went out, it returned with the olive branch. The olive branch denotes the Spirit of God bringing life and peace to the soul. Jesus is the Branch Man in Jeremiah 33, Zechariah 6, and John 15. And the olive branch also symbolizes the anointing, for there is oil in the olive branch. Every time the Dove of God comes, he brings fresh oil for the sons and daughters of the Most High!

The Dove, the Holy Spirit, cannot rest where there is corruption and death. For generations the Dove sought a place to rest. It flew over Abraham, Moses, and the Prophets until at last at the River Jordan, the Dove came from the open heaven and rested on the perfect man, Jesus, the Son of God (Matthew 3:16).

A third time the dove flew from the ark, and like on the day of Pentecost, the world was ready for the abiding presence of the Dove! Finally there was a place now ready in the hearts of men for the Dove to rest. He has come not as a fluttering guest but as the abiding presence. He has come to build a nest in the hearts of men. Has the gentle Dove found a nest in your heart?

LET'S PRAY

Lord Jesus, I love you! Thank you for sending me the power and revelation of your Holy Spirit. I want more. Please shower me with your grace today to know you intimately. I want to flow in the life of the Spirit and bring forth fruit, sweet fruit, for others to taste. Give me grace to walk every moment of this day with you, filled with your Spirit! Amen.

27

GOD'S COVENANT
WITH NOAH

*Noah erected an altar dedicated to Yahweh. Then he selected
ritually clean animals and birds of every species and offered them
as burnt sacrifices on the altar. And when Yahweh smelled the
sweet fragrance of Noah's offerings, his heart was stirred, and
he said: "Never again will I curse the earth because of people,
even though I know the imagination of their hearts is evil from
childhood; nor will I ever again destroy every living creature as
I have done. I promise this:
As long as earth exists there will always be seasons of planting and
harvest, cold and heat, summer and winter, day and night."*

GENESIS 8:20–22

Can you imagine what it would have been like to spend a year on a houseboat? And with all the smells of those animals? That's how long Noah spent in the ark. Five months floating and seven months on the mountain. God give us the patience of Noah! Noah did not stir until God spoke to him. This man was obedient to God, refusing to move until he heard the word of the Lord. Just as he waited for the command to enter, he waited for the command to disembark. Faith will wait until God speaks. Finding grace in God's eyes does not free us to do as we please. We must wait for the voice of the Lord and his timing. We are under his government.

God will remember you just like he remembered his floating menagerie. He watches to see that we have been faithful, even in the "confined place" in which he has placed us. The word "remembered" in reference to Noah in Genesis 8:1 means "marked." Noah was a marked man, and so are we!

Noah and his family would never forget the moment they pushed open the door of the ark and walked out into a new world. Eight human beings found a new beginning with God. Like a new Adam and a new Eve, they began all over again. What a spine-tingling moment it must have been! The bright sunlight, the fresh air, the gentle breeze . . . God had seen them through! And the mountain they landed on? It was Ararat, the Hebrew word for "the curse is reversed!" They landed in a realm where the curse was broken and blessings flowed again!

NOAH BUILDS AN ALTAR

The first thing Noah did when he got out of the ark was to worship Yahweh. Noah realized the great love of God that was upon his life and offered himself to God. God is always ready to renew a relationship with people when they turn to him. All alone as a family in a cold and desolate world, Noah did not build a house; he built an altar, the first altar in Scripture. In humble gratitude, he worshipped at the altar as he offered sacrifices to God. The true worshipper gives thanks after escaping catastrophe. God accepts our worship when mercy pierces our heart.

This sacrifice was an act of praise and submission to God. And as the smoke of the sacrifice curled up into the approving blue sky, God was pleased. Noah realized God's fixed purpose is to bring man from sin into righteousness based on sacrifice. Noah confessed the evil that was in him and, like Abel, brought a pleasing sacrifice to God. Elohim started the human race over with this worshipping community.

Noah sacrificed burnt offerings from the stock of clean animals that came off the ark. God viewed this sacrifice as a "sweet fragrance . . . and His heart was stirred" (v. 21). The Hebrew word for sweet fragrance can mean "an aroma of rest." This sacrifice caused the Father to rest. It satisfied and stirred the Father. And so, God declares that he would never again destroy man or beast completely.

The flood was so painful to God, and Noah's sacrifice so beautiful, that it moved the Father's heart to make a covenant with man forever. God has pity toward mankind even though their imagination is evil from their youth (Psalm 78:38–39; 103:8–14). God reveals his mercy by this covenant with mankind. As long as the earth exists, God will faithfully provide for man through all our seasons and all our days. Grace is greater than our sin. Mercy triumphs over judgment.

This covenant promise of God was based on sacrifice (Genesis 8:20–22; Ephesians 5:2). The annual fulfillment of this covenant through the centuries forms a striking demonstration of God's faithfulness. A covenant is an oath of promise made between God and man. There are seven covenants God makes in Scripture:

1. God's covenant with Adam (Genesis 3)

2. God's covenant with Noah (8–9)

3. God's covenant with Abraham (15)

4. God's covenant with Moses and Israel (Exodus 20–34)

5. God's covenant with Levi and the priesthood (Numbers 25; Ezekiel 44:15; Malachi 2:4–5)

6. God's covenant with David (2 Samuel 23)

7. God's new covenant with his church, ratified by his blood (Matthew 26:28)

After living in the ark for a year, Noah's life involved an altar and a tent. He didn't build a city but an altar. He didn't build a house but lived in a tent. Noah's tent with the altar outside was a preview of the coming tabernacle with the altar for the burnt offering. God lived with Noah in his tent.

"God lovingly blessed Noah and all his family" (Genesis 9:1). The days of Noah remind us of the days surrounding the return of our Lord Jesus (Matthew 24:37–39). Yet the "days of Noah" also include his days in the ark and his days of blessing as he disembarks from the floating covenant-house. Noah became the ruler of the world. God gave a whole new world to the one whom the world once persecuted, maligned, and misunderstood. So shall it be in the last days: God will give his people the authority over this world. God will give the media, government, science, and the arts back to the last days' generation of awakeners. The church will emerge as the regents of the planet.

God blessed Noah and his sons as the new heads of humanity. And the human race began again with the blessing and good will of God upon their lives. Noah's offering on the altar of sacrifice brought God's response of blessing and his covenant grace. A new era of human existence began with this charter covenant God gave to Noah:

- God commanded them to reproduce, be fruitful, and to populate the earth.

- Noah received power over the animals.

- God granted permission to eat the flesh of living creatures. Every creature of God is now good for food, and we are to refuse nothing (1 Timothy 4:4).

Evidently, prior to the flood, man was a vegetarian. Since Noah spared all the animals by placing them in the ark, and all the animals owe their lives to humankind, God allowed Noah to take the lives of animals for food. Every time we eat meat, we should remember that we are living because an animal gave its life. It's almost as if God gives us meat as food to remind us that physically we live by the death of another and spiritually we live by the death of another. We live spiritually because God's Son gave his life for us by shedding his blood.

LET'S PRAY

Jesus, you gave your life for me. Now, I give my life for you. Everything I have and everything I own is yours. My family, my hopes, my expectations, my dreams—I lay them at your feet this day. I pledge my soul to heaven. I want to live only and always for you. Make my life a clear picture of what God's love can do for one who loves you. Amen.

28

THE RAINBOW COVENANT

When the rainbow is in the clouds,
I will see it and remember the everlasting covenant.

GENESIS 9:16

Who doesn't like the sight of a beautiful rainbow after the storm? Imagine the delight Noah and his family felt as they gazed upon God's signature in the sky. God's covenant is that a worldwide flood will never again destroy the earth (Isaiah 54:9). The seal or signature of this covenant was the rainbow in the clouds. This "bow" is without arrows. The unstrung bow in the sky is a sign of peace and freedom that God hangs over the human race. The bow in the clouds was not only a promise that God would not destroy the earth with a flood, but it was a token of a new relationship.

"I will see it," God declared as he put a rainbow in the clouds for you. God is light, and the rainbow is the light and glory of God revealed in faithfulness to mankind. The rainbow is the reflection of the beams of the sun, showing the excellency of this covenant as it streams from the glory of the "sun of righteousness" (Malachi 4:2; Ezekiel 1:28; Revelation 4:3, 11).

The seven colors of the rainbow represent the fullness of the Spirit or the seven-fold manifestation appearing in the earth (Revelation 4:5).

Purple – Royalty: Jesus is the King (1 Timothy 6:15).

Blue – Heaven: Jesus came from heaven (John 3:13).

Green – New life: Jesus gives life to us all (14:6).

Yellow – Brightness of the sun: Jesus is light (8:12).

Orange – The amber glow of glory: Jesus is the glory (Ezekiel 1:27).

Red – Blood: The blood of Jesus washes away sin (Revelation 1:5).

God hung up his battle bow to be a sign of peace. For his covenant with man turned judgment into grace. He remembers his covenant, not our sin! This is the sweet message of "no accusing voice of condemnation against those who are joined in life-union with Jesus, the Anointed One" (Romans 8:1). The bow points up, not down to the guilty ones!

But now we have a covenant better than a rainbow: the precious promises of Christ! His grace can take the storm clouds and teardrops of our lives and turn them into arches of triumph and glorious jewels. The half-arch of the rainbow will one day become a full circle going around the throne (Revelation 4:3). Only those in the glory can see the full rainbow of his throne.

When God sees the rainbow, he will remember his forever-covenant! It's not my remembering God, but it's God remembering me. It's not my laying hold of his covenant, but his covenant lays hold of me. Glory be to God! We might forget him, but our Lord cannot forget us. He has written us upon on the palms of his hands.

When I look to Jesus, it brings me joy and peace. But it's God looking to Jesus that secures my salvation and that of all his elect. For you see, it's impossible for our God to be angry with us when he sees Christ's blood. His covenant of love is not of man, neither by man, but the Lord's alone. It's God's remembering us, not our remembering him, that secures the everlasting covenant.

The blood given to ratify the new covenant overshadows all the covenants of the Old Testament. However, the prophets of the Old Testament did refer to the Noahic covenant. Notice how they use similar language as that found in Genesis 9:

"To me, this is like the time
when I vowed that the waters of Noah's flood
would never again cover the earth.
Now I vow to you that I will neither be angry with you
nor rebuke you.
Even if the mountains were to crumble and the hills
disappear,
my heart of steadfast faithful love will never leave you,
and my covenant of peace with you will never be shaken,"
says Yahweh, whose love and compassion will never give
up on you. (Isaiah 54:9–10)

THE SIN OF NOAH

Noah, a farmer, was the first to plant a vineyard. He
drank so much of the wine he made that he got drunk
and passed out naked inside his tent. And Ham, the
father of Canaan, went into the tent and gazed on
his shamefully exposed father. Then he went out and
informed his brothers. (Genesis 9:20–22)

Noah had been a carpenter while building the ark. After the
flood, he became a farmer. In the first garden, Adam fell, and in
the second garden, Noah fell. He harvested grapes and called a
celebration of feasting with his family. His sin was not just that he
got drunk and forgot to put his clothes on. The Hebrew text infers
that it was a deliberate act of nudity. Some scholars conclude that
Ham's sin was homosexual activity with his father. Interestingly,
Moses, the author of Genesis, seems to keep the details of this sin
private, and perhaps we should learn a lesson from that also. We
are all a fallen people, regardless of how many blessings we have.
Man is unable to stand without grace. Even though Noah found
grace for his salvation from the flood, he still needed to find grace
to live a life that honors God.

Notice the similarity between Adam and Noah:

- They both came forth after the earth emerged from
  water (Genesis 1:12).

- God made them both lords over creation (v. 28).

- God blessed them both and told them to multiply (v. 28).

- They both worked in a garden.

- Their temptations and falls from grace both occurred in a garden/vineyard.

- Both their sins resulted in nakedness (3:7).

- Someone else covered their nakedness.

- Their sin brought a great curse to their descendants.

- After their sin, both received a prophecy of redemption.

- Both had three sons.

Ham sinned by not covering his naked father. To expose and sneer at his father's fall was wickedness of the worst kind. Ham failed to honor his father and lacked covering love (1 Peter 4:8). Had he really cared for his father, he would have covered him with the robe of honor as did Shem and Japheth.

The sin nature of humanity loves to see those in authority exposed to shame, for it gives them a false freedom from restriction and gives them an excuse for their own sin. The failure of Noah becomes a test for his sons. The failures of our leaders test our response. Apart from Jesus Christ, there are no perfect leaders, only imperfect. Your boss, your pastor, your best friend, your mother and father . . . all are imperfect. When we expose those over us to dishonor and humiliation, it brings a curse. Proverbs 30:17 states, "The eye that mocks his father and dishonors his elderly mother deserves to be plucked out by the ravens of the valley and fed to the young vultures!" On the other hand, Shem and Japheth exhibited love and respect for their father along with an understanding of God's method of dealing with human nakedness. Because they covered their father, they inherited a blessing.

Noah's prophecy over Shem was that Yahweh would now be the God of Shem in a unique way, mingling his name with Shem's

(Shem means "name"). This is a prophecy that a descendant of Shem would be Yahweh incarnate. Jesus Christ descended from Shem! Shem's reward was that he would be the ancestor of Christ. Noah blesses the God of Shem as the Covenant Keeper. The descendants of Japheth may have enlargement (Genesis 9:27), but Shem has God.

Interestingly, all three sons of Noah were generationally present at the crucifixion of the Lord Jesus. The descendants of Shem were present in the Jewish religious leaders who wanted the Messiah dead and out of the way. Japheth was present in the Romans who participated jointly with the Jews to crucify the Lord Jesus. And a descendant of Ham was present in the person of Simon of Cyrene, who bore the cross of Christ in servitude (Luke 23:26).

The Bible brings the sons of Noah before us again in Acts 8–10. The Ethiopian eunuch was a descendant of Ham and received the blessing of the gospel (Acts 8). Saul of Tarsus (Paul) was a descendant of Shem and converted after the revelation of Jesus (Acts 9). Cornelius the centurion was a son of Japheth who believed the good news of Christ (Acts 10).

Let's Pray

Father-God, you have blessed me. The power of the cross of your Son Jesus has broken every curse. You have set me free from generational curses, the curses of others, and from every curse I have spoken over myself. Freedom is mine because of your great love for me. I thank you today that I will walk in the Spirit of life and in the freedom from every curse. Your name is great and greatly to be praised! Amen.

29

NIMROD

Nimrod, a mighty despot before Yahweh.

GENESIS 10:9

The Bible introduces the man Nimrod as an Ethiopian, whose name means "rebel." He grew to be a mighty warrior on the earth, the first of the heroic conquerors. But Nimrod was ambitious, aspiring to be over others. This self-promoting spirit controlled him. Walking in pride and tyranny, he soon became a "mighty hunter" before the Lord. This implies he was a violent invader of others' rights and properties.

Nimrod was a terrorist. The Septuagint text reads, "He was a mighty hunter against the Lord." As a terrorist, Nimrod became a powerful ruler over others, laying the foundations of a monarchy.

He had no God-given right or command to rule. He simply took it upon himself to govern by fear and force.

The Hebrew word used here for "mighty" means "chief" or "chieftain." He was the most outstanding leader in the four hundred years between the flood and Abraham. Nimrod was also a man who developed false worship (Babel). Babylonia was long known as the "Land of Nimrod."

Nimrod built a kingdom, a kingdom of this world, and ruled over the construction of cities. His one aim was to make a name for himself. His ambition was to make a worldwide kingdom for himself. What a destructive spirit this is when released among men! It can destroy a church, even nations.

THE TOWER OF BABEL

"Now everyone at that time spoke a single language with one vocabulary" (Genesis 11:1). As the descendants of Noah multiplied, the earth filled with a people of one language. The people likely used this common language to worship the Creator and sing his praises. But sadly, they also misused God's gift of language.

As men moved westward (turning their backs on the sunrise), they found a plain in Shinar or "Babylon." And they dwelt there together as one in what we know as Iraq. This is the place where they built a tower of bricks, and this brick tower was for the worship of pagan deities. It was around this tower that the ambitious Nimrod united them as one empire. Once again, man became defiant of God.

Nimrod was not just content to build numerous cities, but he sought to build one that would tower above them all. This pagan metropolis was a vain attempt to deify man and his accomplishments. The people didn't want to be scattered and were defiant of

God's command to "populate the earth" (9:1). The sons of Noah had traded their tents for townhouses.

Just as Lucifer sought to exalt himself above the heavens, so fallen men seek to build their own towers into the heavens. Babel-builders still exist today, striving to do the same thing. Man is ambitious, seeking his own greatness. We erect our cities, our systems of commerce, even religious institutions. Yet at the heart of many of these towers is selfish ambition, the desire to make our own names great and deny the greatness of God's name.

An ancient historian, Philo Judaeus, describes that day in which each person in Babel engraved their names upon the bricks to memorialize themselves. Today, no one remembers their names, but the name of God stands as a high tower.

Seeking to make a name for ourselves is self-worship. This is totally contrary to scripture; we're to lay aside our reputation to make the name of Jesus famous (Philippians 2:3–11). Jesus made himself of no reputation, so why would we seek to make our names great (Jeremiah 45:5)? Babel means "confusion," and every Babel we erect will result in confusion.

Nowhere in the Bible is there any mention of the Shinar people seeking God or waiting upon him for direction. Out of the ambitious schemes of man, this tower of confusion arose. Babylon is a picture of this world system that has no room for the living God.

The Lord went down to see the city and the tower the people had built for themselves, just like he did when he came in human form. Jesus Christ, the Son of God, came down to this earth to see the works of our lives and carry our judgment to his cross (Psalm 113:5–6). God came to Babylon to frustrate this worldwide conspiracy to unite the nations of the earth under one government. He came to "look at every proud man and bring them low" (Job 40:11–14).

On top of the tower and on its ceiling and walls were star charts and the signs of the zodiac. Scholars and encyclopedias agree that astrology began in Babylon. Behind the four-footed beasts, behind the birds, behind the men, lurked the real host of the heavens whose leader is the daystar, Lucifer. The purpose of the tower was to worship the stars, the host of heaven. Eventually an elite group of priests and priestesses developed. This select group was the only one with the knowledge of how to worship the stars. They began to include sexual mythology in their worship. The priestesses became prostitutes, and the priests became male prostitutes. By the time of Joshua, the land of Canaan had grown into full-blown Baalism.

Like Nimrod, Pharaoh of Egypt made his treasury cities out of bricks. Out of their rebellion, they decided to erect a city from what their hands could make. A city made by man. But God's building will never include bricks, only stones. Man makes clay bricks, but God is the maker of living stones—the living stones that will make up the city of God, the New Jerusalem (Revelation 21:18–20).

Soon we will see this eternal city, a city not made by hands! The church is built together with the living stones of those who love the Lord Jesus. And we will see the New Jerusalem emerge, the city that is a bride.

God's judgment of Babel resulted in the confusion of their language. God released thousands of different languages, and confusion reigned. Men and women would think in one language and use another because God had changed their brain centers and their vocal cords.

Perhaps, they each thought that others were mocking them. For soon fighting began that would reach the point where those who spoke the same language got together and said, "Let's leave. We can't live here any longer." They began to scatter. One small group stayed behind near Ur of the Chaldees. This is where we pick up the genealogy in our story.

The multitude of languages today is a monument to sin. Unity in the Spirit of God brings a common speech, which is Jesus the Word, the language of God! Pentecost reversed this judgment. The nations of the earth heard each man speaking in their own languages as the Holy Spirit enabled them (Acts 2). One day, all languages will gather around the Lamb on the throne in glorified praise to him.

Let's Pray

Heavenly Father, your name is glorious! I want you to use me today. Take my life and use me to show others how wonderful and how kind you are. I surrender my time, my talents, and my treasure to you. I don't want to build something that you will destroy. I want to build your kingdom. I want everything I do today to be filled with your pleasure and accomplished by the power of your Spirit. Amen.

30

The Generations from the Flood to Abram

So Yahweh scattered them over the entire earth.

Genesis 11:8

Genesis is filled with amazing details. In Genesis 11 we discover that people lived so much longer than they do in our present day. We can note the decreasing life span of those individuals listed in this chapter: Shem lived 600 years, Arphaxad 438, Salah 433, Peleg 239 years, Serug 230, and Nahor 148. Some suggest that perhaps this is because of the disappearance of the vapor canopy that once covered the earth before the flood.

From Shem to Abraham, we cover ten generations (427 years from the flood to Abraham). Noah died two years before Abraham was born. Note the mention of Eber (v. 14), whose name is the root word for "Hebrew." At last we come to Terah and his three sons—Abram, Nahor, and Haran, the father of Lot and grandfather of Rebekah.

> Here are the descendants of Terah: Terah was the
> father of Abram, Nahor, and Haran, and Haran was the
> father of Lot. Haran preceded his father, Terah, in death
> in the land of his birth, in the Chaldean city of Ur. The
> brothers, Abram and Nahor were both married. Abram's
> wife was Sarai. Nahor married the daughter of his
> deceased brother Haran; her name was Milcah, and her
> sister was Iscah. Now Sarai was barren and childless.
>
> Terah took his son Abram, his grandson Lot, the son
> of Haran, and his daughter-in-law Sarai, his son Abram's
> wife, and they all departed together from the Chaldean
> city Ur to go into the land of Canaan. But when they
> journeyed as far as Haran, they settled there. Terah lived
> 205 years and died in Haran. (11:27–32)

The family home of Terah was Ur of the Chaldeans, a major city located north of the Persian Gulf. At 2000 BCE, it was the greatest city in the world. The word Chaldea means "demonic," and Ur means "flame." Ur was an ancient city-state in Mesopotamia (modern Iraq). You can still see the ruin of Ur at modern Tell el-Muqayyar. In 2000 BCE, Ur was perhaps one of the largest cities of the world. It is clear that Abram and his father served foreign gods. Ur was named after the moon goddess and was the center of her worship. The Chaldeans were astrologers, occultists, and idol worshippers. Ancient traditions state that Terah was an idol-maker until his death. While the family clan was still in Ur, Haran died, leaving Lot fatherless. While still in Ur, Abram married Sarai (Sarah), and she remained barren for many years to come.

Jewish writers have a tradition that Abram was cast into a fiery furnace for refusing to worship idols and miraculously survived. God snatched him as a stick out of the burning fire!

It was from this man Abram that the nations were born. This is just the beginning of our story! From the loins of Adam to the loins of Abraham will come a people who know their God, a people who know their destiny, a people who walk in unity and in love! God made mankind in his own image, and now his people will display that image once again on this earth. From the first Adam to the last Adam, the story will be complete as we arise the pure spotless bride, displaying his image as God destined it to be!

When we believe in Jesus Christ, we become a true spiritual "seed" of Abraham. Believers today are inheritors of the promises and blessings of Abraham. We can thank our Jewish friends for our spiritual lineage. As spiritual sons and daughters of the living God, we live blessed lives. The moment we believe, God lavishes upon us every blessing heaven contains. To understand all that our Father has given us in Christ is life's sacred quest. Nothing can hinder God's blessings when we walk daily in the love of Christ.

Today, step into the blessings God has for your life. Appropriate them by faith and watch them manifest in your home, your career, and your ministry. God will use you, like he did Abraham, to raise up others who will walk in God's ways. The Lord is ready and able to meet you and empower you to walk in his ways.

LET'S PRAY

My loving Father, thank you for all your works, for they are glorious! Your work of creation takes my breath away. Your wonderful grace is my strength and confidence. And the mercy that you show me when I fail you is my hope and glory. Thank you for the book of beginnings, the firstfruits of your creative power. Continue to bring forth in me the purpose of my life. I want to make you happy, and I want to make a difference on the earth. Walk with me today, in Jesus's Name. Amen.

To be continued . . .

ENDNOTES

1   Three is the number of resurrection (Hosea 6:2–3).

2   The believer is birthed by the Divine Seed, God's Word (1 Peter 1:23; James 1:18).

3   Also in regeneration, those who were dead in sins have been raised to walk in newness of life (Ephesians 2:1–9; Romans 6:1–11).

4   In Genesis 1:26, the plural form of the verb indicates there were more being(s) than Father-God in the activities of creation. When taken as a whole, the Bible also points to the Holy Spirit and God the Son as participators in the glory of creation. See Psalm 104:30; John 1:1–3; Hebrews 1:1–3.

5   In Genesis 1:26, the translation could read "as our image" rather than "in our image." Image can also be translated "representation, resemblance." God created someone like himself to reflect who he is into all his creation. He created trees after their

kind, birds after their kind, fish after their kind, and animals after their kind, but now he creates a God-kind of being. Man and woman will resemble him and bring his image into the created order. Christ is the image of God (Romans 8:29; 1 Corinthians 11:7; 2 Corinathians 3:18; 4:4; Colossians 1:15; 3:10; Hebrews 1:3). The first man, Adam, was a type or figure of the last Adam, Christ. See Romans 5:14; 1 Corinthians 15:40–58.

6   In Psalm 8:5, the Hebrew word used in other translations is "heavenly beings," but it is actually "Elohim," the Creator.

7   The servant Father: the Hebrew word "blessed" means to "kneel before someone in the attitude of servanthood." We have a God who touches his creation and breathes into man his breath, kneeling to serve the creation he formed.

8   The Hebrew word for day is yom and can be translated in English into over fifty different words, such as "a twenty-four hour day, today, time, forever, continually, age, life, season, perpetually, a period of time."

9   Literally, the "breath of lives" (life and the power to procreate).

10   *Havilah has a number of possible meanings: "to cause to grow, to give birth out of pain, a stretch of sandy land, mud, t*o twist or whirl in a circular or spiral manner (to writhe or fall grievously in pain or fear), to grieve, be sore pained, be sorrowful, tremble, be wounded." All of the possible meanings seem to point to our human nature. The overflowing increase of God's river within us uncovers the gold hidden in the mud.

11   It was four thousand years later when the Virgin Mary gave birth to a child whose name Jesus means "Jehovah, the Savior."

12   In Genesis 4:11, blood-guilt not only stains the conscience but it also defiles the ground. See Numbers 35:33. We are told to avoid the way of Cain (Jude 11), which would include (1) offering God what is cursed, (2) jealous anger toward another, (3) refusing to repent, (4) murder, and (5) wandering away from God's presence.

13   That is, seven times over—seven lives will be taken to avenge Cain's death. Or it could mean seven generations will be avenged. The next murderer we find in Scripture is Lamech, seventh generation from Cain. Jewish sages believe it was Lamech who killed his ancestor Cain.

14   In Genesis 4:21, "instruments" may refer to "the harp (stringed instrument) and flute (wind instrument)." The Hebrew word play means "to hold, to handle," and later became associated with "to play skillfully." Jubal invented musical instruments and taught others to play them. See Job 21:12; 30:31. Musicians today should dedicate their gifts and talents to God for heaven to be glorified.

15   In Genesis 5:21, Methuselah is a complex name with at least two words embedded within it: "death" and "send/let go." Some scholars believe his name means "when he dies, it will be sent" or "his death will bring." This is a prophecy hidden in his name, for the year he died was the year God sent the flood. Jewish writers say that Methuselah, Noah's grandfather, died seven days before the flood and that Noah and his family entered the ark the day Methuselah died (7:10). An alternate meaning of Methuselah is "man of the spear (weapon)."

16   The Hebrew word is "Adam"—humankind.

17   See Job 1:6; 2:1; 4:18–19; 38:7; Dead Sea scrolls 1QapGen, 4QDtj, and 4QDtq; the Damascus Document 4Q180; the Book of Jubilees; 2 Baruch; the Book of Enoch; the Jewish historian Josephus; and church fathers Justin Martyr, Eusebius, Clement of Alexandria, and Origen.

18   "Pitch" is a gummy, sticky substance that waterproofs the ark. Interestingly, this is not the word usually used for pitch. The Old Testament uses this word seventy times to mean "atonement."

About the Authors

Dr. Brian Simmons is a passionate lover of God. After a dramatic conversion to Christ, Brian knew that God was calling him to go to the unreached people of the world and present the gospel of God's grace to all who would listen. With his wife Candice and their three children, he spent eight years in the tropical rain forest of the Darien Province of Panama as a church planter, translator, linguist, and consultant. Brian assisted in the Paya-Kuna New Testament translation project. After their ministry in the jungle, Brian was instrumental in planting a thriving church in New England (U.S.) and now travels full time as a speaker and Bible teacher. He is currently the lead translator for The Passion Translation Project, which will produce a new, dynamic version of the Bible that promises to shape the spirituality of coming generations. He has been happily married to Candice for forty-eight years and is known to boast regularly of his three children, six grandchildren, and three great-grandchildren.